EIR (ISSN 0273-6314) *is published weekly (50 issues), by EIR News Service, Inc., P.O. Box 17390, Washington, D.C. 20041-0390. (703) 777-9451*

European Headquarters: E.I.R. GmbH, Postfach Bahnstrasse 9a, D-65205, Wiesbaden, Germany Tel: 49-611-73650
Homepage: http://www.eirna.com
e-mail: eirna@eirna.com
Director: Georg Neudecker

Montreal, Canada: 514-461-1557

Denmark: EIR - Danmark, Sankt Knuds Vej 11, basement left, DK-1903 Frederiksberg, Denmark. Tel.: +45 35 43 60 40, Fax: +45 35 43 87 57. e-mail: eirdk@hotmail.com.

Mexico City: EIR, Sor Juana Inés de la Cruz 242-2 Col. Agricultura C.P. 11360 Delegación M. Hidalgo, México D.F. Tel. (5525) 5318-2301
eirmexico@gmail.com

Canada Post Publication Sales Agreement #40683579

Postmaster: Send all address changes to *EIR*, P.O. Box 17390, Washington, D.C. 20041-0390.

Signed articles in *EIR* represent the views of the authors, and not necessarily those of the Editorial Board.

Rebuilding the World In the BRICS Era

EIR Contents

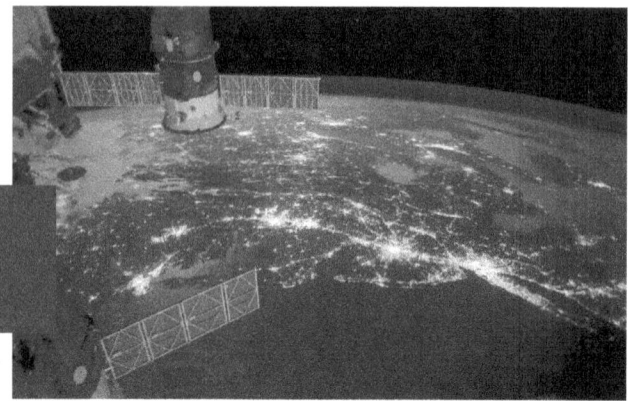

NASA

Cover This Week

Mankind's development on the Earth and beyond Image

II. BRICS BREAKTHROUGH IN PARIS

The Schiller Institute held a large and successful event, to bring Europe into the new paradigm of the BRICS nations. Diplomats, economists, business people, and citizens from Eurasian and African nations took part.

Again, the Case of Germany's Role

by Lyndon LaRouche

EIR *Founding Editor Lyndon LaRouche gave the following analysis at a strategy discussion June 9, after German Chancellor Angela Merkel had agreed to Obama's policy of excluding Russia from the "G7 Summit":*

Let's start with a very significant issue; again which pertains to the German situation. It pertains to the argument that I presented as part of our team on Monday; that the three senior members of the German team [former Chancellors Helmut Schmidt and Gerhard Schröder, and current Foreign Minister Frank-Walter Steinmeier—ed.], who are partly technically in retreat, but are actually quite active. German policy works that way.

But the issue is simple; there's only one nation in Western Europe which has any actual, efficient integrity in economy, and that is Germany. The German economy is still an efficient economy in structure; it has a certain amount of garbage accumulated from the so-called left wing—the wild wing, or whatever. But you have three active leaders in the German organization; two of whom are technically retired (but that doesn't mean much), and one who is the active leader. And so what they've done is, they've laid out a policy which is a challenge to Merkel; a direct challenge to her. Which would mean that Germany would tell Merkel, "Stop the shit! And you are not going to have Germany excluding Russia, because Russia is a part of Europe; the Russian economy is a part of Europe, it's a very good part of Europe. It's one of the strongest parts of Europe."

One of the strongest forces of Europe is the German economy. Although the German economy has been suffering the effects of other things along the line; and therefore, the pressure on them has been increasing. And this increase threatens to destroy the functional integrity of the German economy.

The French economy is very poor; the Italian economy is more or less shattered. Spain and Portugal are almost nonexistent in terms of being nations as such; even though the Spanish used to have a great railway system, relatively speaking, but there's not much left of anything else there.

So, the point is this; Germany cannot continue to accept the rate of collapse of the actually efficient part of the German economy. Because otherwise, Germany

German Chancellor Angela Merkel with her Foreign Minister Frank-Walter Steinmeier, February 13, 2013.

Bundesregierung/Bergmann

would become as rotten as most of Western Europe is. This includes France and Italy and so forth; they are not competent systems. They've been broken down before then, and how this breakdown occurred is a matter of history, so we don't need to go through it here. But that's the fact. Germany is the only nation in Europe, outside of Russia, which has any real integrity as a functional economy.

Merkel the Problem

The others? Take the case of our own United States.

What do we produce in our own United States in terms of economy? Less than bullshit. The skills of our people have been driven to a level, where they are practically non-functional. If they had any functional potentials, they're denied the use of them. And there are very few exceptions to that; and it's only a sprinkling of exceptions of specialists, like certain machinists' institutions and things like that, which are significant. But they're highly withdrawn; they're contracted, because the U.S. economy is disintegrating and has been disintegrating at an accelerating rate.

So therefore, Germany is the only economy in this particular sector, in terms of the northern quarters, the only one that has actual integrity as an economy. France does not; Spain has lost it a long time ago. We don't even talk about some other places; they're gone.

And so therefore, the issue is rather complex, but it's fun. First of all, if Germany is allowed by itself to open up an active economic policy relationship with Russia, then the Russian economy is strengthened; and the German economy is protected against an imminent systematic disintegration, where it goes into the also-ran category of most of the rest of Western Europe.

So this is the reality; and the problem is Merkel. As long as Merkel has any control with her policies over the German economy, the German economy will be soon plunging into the dismal condition of the other parts of Western and Central Europe. And that's the situation.

Now, the other part of the thing is, again: If Germany is able to function in trade relations on technology, production, then you cannot have a war between Germany and Russia, or war-like situation. In that case, the whole thing is jammed up; and Obama and all these other things get into jeopardy. Because look at where China is; China is the most powerful nation in terms of personnel on the planet. It has the highest rate of technological progress of any nation on the planet. The United States is a pinko, relative to what China represents today in terms of technology.

Will U.S. Destroy Itself?

But this is what *we* are! Because everything that we are concerned about, in the United States in particular, depends upon these kinds of considerations that I've just mentioned. And it represents it in two respects: Will the United States destroy itself? Because if it goes to war, it will be destroying itself; as well as bringing down a lot of other nations in general warfare.

So, there is no possibility of a capitulation to what Obama represents, or what most of Wall Street represents, in particular. The British Empire, without this kind of control, is really weak; it's a failure, it'll disintegrate. There's nothing much there; the whole British sector is disintegrating, and it should. And the disintegration is, why? It's not because somebody said "Let's do this, or let's do that." Actually, the British population is not competent to live; and a lot of other parts of Europe have lost the competence to live. They can't maintain themselves; they can't cope with the threats that reality presents to them.

That defines what our policy has to be; which is the point I presented, together with our team, on Monday. That's our policy. And our policy is, we have to get rid of Obama; we have to get rid of the Wall Street crowd, which throwing out Obama will do.

So, all the other talk about this and that, and this could be and that might be, and this might be, is all nonsense. Forget it! Don't even mention it anymore. You're wasting time and distracting attention. We're now at a point where we're coming to a point of crisis; where the world is coming into a point where everything is coming into a common point of consideration. Not a scattered bunch of points, but one concentrated point. That point is, on the one hand, going to thermonuclear war; thermonuclear war means the extermination of the human species.

But, you say, "Well, we won't do that." "Well, how are you going to stop it? How are you going to prevent it? It's almost now." If Obama continues as President, it probably will happen; and it probably will happen within as soon as weeks, or maybe a couple of months. And when it happens, you're all dead. *That's the issue!* All this other stuff is just peripheral gossip. This is the issue which is now a global issue; defining the fate of mankind globally, with one big fell swoop.

And war, when it goes off—if it does go off—ain't gonna take long to go. Thermonuclear warfare under present modern conditions. General warfare? Nah.

By Contrast, John Kennedy

We almost hit that, as has been noticed again and again, in the Soviet threat on Cuba. The Cuba crisis with Kennedy. What President Kennedy prevented, with his brother, working together; created the last stage of the Soviet Union to withhold, to destroy its thermonuclear weapon system. And they did it; and if you had the right seasoning, you get up there and watch, the explosion, the great black and fiery motions going over northern Russia, the backlands. Boom, boom, boom; going for weeks. Firing off these weapons; weapons which could have wiped out the United States. And they didn't. Why? Because of John F. Kennedy, knew how to handle this problem, he and his brother. And he and his brother did the job.

President John Kennedy during his speech to the nation on the Cuban Missile crisis, October 24, 1962.

So, you're in a situation like that time. You can't say, "Well, this part of the planet, and this part of the planet, and this part of the planet, are different parts of the planet." Bunk! We have a global system, a global threat, a global process, and we have to take account of that. Now what that means is, you're not going to have nations as such engaged in war against nations as such. That is no longer a feasible process. Either you have extermination war, or you don't. And what happened, when the Soviet system blew up, the Soviet weapons system under Khrushchov, was a touch point; the model for the extermination of mankind. And what the situation is now is *way beyond* anything like that.

So therefore, what we do, you say, "Well, we're only a small organization." That's nonsense; we have more brains than these guys do. Or at least I know something about that. Our conceptions are competent. The conceptions of Wall Street? Wall Street has no competence whatsoever. If Wall Street has to run an economy, the people of that nation will die. It's inevitable; because they're cannibals. And what do canni-

bals eat? Human beings.

So therefore, the idea that you have a practical solution, or a practical option, or this sort of thing, is a pure mythology; it beats the stupidity of people who don't know any better. And unfortunately, most of the classes of students of universities and so forth today—forget the other schools—the universities, they're traps. The typical mentality of the person at the university level, is absolutely systemically incompetent. They can't do anything that's needed in general. A relative handful of people inside the United States are capable of doing anything.

So therefore, these kinds of considerations and the relationship between Germany's situation, its effect within the European system as well as Russia; the effect that this has on larger parts of the planet integrally, including China, including India, including all the nations of South America, for example. Most of the nations of Asia are nations which are immediately threatened by any development of this nature. This means that mankind has to have a new conception of mankind. All the old so-called practical expositions are nonsense.

Defend the Existence of Mankind

Now this is what we touched on in the discussion on this matter on Monday. And it has to be carried further, because it's crucial now. If we could pull off—

Kremlin.ru

Former German Chancellor Gerhard Schröder with President Putin in Moscow on May 9, 2005.

and we don't have the power to do it—but if we know what it could be; we have a good idea of what to do to make it, should be. And that is, get Merkel either thrown out of office, or subdued totally; let the three chief exponents of the Russian system negotiate the system.

Russia is the only economy in Europe which has any inherent utility, in Western Europe at all. So if Germany, which is the only functional part of a modern economy in that part of Europe, if they are enabled to conduct trade, a system of trade voluntarily in development, technological progress, with Russia. It doesn't mean they have to make any big deal; all they have to do is say, "We are trading with each other once again." Doing that is sufficient, to stabilize all of Europe; because if Germany were to flop, all of Europe would disintegrate. It's already ready to disintegrate, and in the process of pre-disintegration.

The sum total of this thing is, that principle does not arise from force. Principle arises from mental powers. It is the human mind and the development of the powers of the human mind which are the only efficient force by which mankind can defend the existence of mankind.

And that is what this policy must be for our organization. All the other stuff, the popular stuff, the interpretations, the explanations of why things happen, and this happens, it's all been garbage. I've been through the whole pit of the thing; it's all garbage.

To run society, you have to run it from the top down.

The top down means the intellectual ability to create a successful society on a general scale. To develop the necessary relations among nations which make the conditions for doing that possible.

In other words, you have to look at history from the top down. And all the fallacies are people who thought about history from their summed-up time, bottom up. And therefore, what we're doing right now, in this organization—I mean look what you get in Wall Street; look at what you see in New York City. Look at what you see in different parts [of the country]. Look at California; look at the government of California. Look at the government of Texas; look at the government of Louisiana; look at the government of Georgia. And look at the government of—yuck, I puke —Virginia. This is all crap! It does not decide the powers of mankind; it's a source of the farces of mankind's experience. And we have to understand that. The idea of being humble; "Well, you don't know anything about this." "I know enough to know you're totally stupid." That's my usual answer for these creeps.

But we have to understand that that's our policy. That was the discussion that we had, effectively, on Monday; and what we circulated during the course of Tuesday, today. That's the issue. And it's what's in the minds of a few people, relatively, always in the history of mankind, that decides what the outcome could become, under stress conditions.

A New Basis for Peace

Like the case of Bismarck. How did the great wars of the Twentieth Century occur? They would never have occurred if Bismarck had still been in charge. And when they got rid of Bismarck, what happened? Bang, bang, bang! Everything began to collapse. The assassinations—the assassination of the President of France, all these other assassinations and things, and little wars and test wars; like the one with Japan, for example. All these wars began to occur. And then one bright day— bang!—and then World War I was suddenly there. We're in a World War I precondition right now. It's not the same kind of conflict, it's not the same terms; but it's the same logic.

Former German Chancellor Gerhard Schröder with President Putin in Moscow on May 9, 2005.

Look at the Twentieth Century. People think that they're smart because they got a Twentieth-Century education. That's the dumbest thing I ever heard! It's a fact. I know this because of my experience with the education system; and I knew very early in life that the education system I was subjected to—both in secondary schools and in universities—was crap. And the principle is exemplified by the fact that there was only one man in the Twentieth Century as a scientist, who was really qualified for physical science as a leader: Albert Einstein. All of the rest of them called themselves great things, had certain degrees of qualified talent, but none of them except Einstein understood the principle of science, of scientific progress. And that's the difference.

And therefore, we have to understand what this organization must be; and how it must make itself self-organized, to the mission which is required. Because you're in your situation, all explanations, all the usual customary practical expositions are just crap. And we've reached the point that all that stuff is way past. What we have is a relationship to China, a relationship to India, a relationship to some South American nations which are now emerging. They're not perfected yet, but they have promise. We see the relationship between China and the South American nations; what their development is, what the promise is. So what we want to do is, establish this kind of peace; which is not really a simple peace where everybody's going to have one-world dreams and so forth. But it's a way in which the nations of the world can organize and interchange

their organizational efforts into a culminating something else.

And when you look at what Ben [Deniston] has had fun with—the Galactic System—and then you go back before the Galactic System was known, to Kepler. The history of mankind is that what most people believe is nonsense. The history of mankind is like the discoveries of Kepler. The discovery of Kepler is that there's a higher order in the Solar System and beyond the Solar System, which is something which began to become known through the work of Kepler. That mankind is a unified process, implicitly. It has different characteristics, but the way it expresses its commonality, is in the convergence of ingenuity. And it's this kind of convergence of ingenuity of different nations and different cultures of a particular time, which is the thing upon which mankind depends.

How are we going to control the galaxy? How are we going to control even the practical system as such, as we have it now? It means we have to organize the relations of mankind, throughout mankind, to meet this challenge. And to bring nations together now, with their different languages, their different habits, and all these kinds of things that go there; and we see what China is showing, and what is otherwise being shown in the process now; and China is the leader in this process. That would develop a relation among nations, and among the peoples of nations, which becomes an efficient means for the commonality of the general interest. It does not mean they have to adopt common things; common habits, common everything; but they have to converge on the efficiency of the common goal.

And that's what we have to understand. And don't get out and try to say, "Well, here, I've got some facts. And these facts are going to tell me the thing is going to work this way." All those kinds of explanations that I know, are crap. Yes, there's divergence in the form in which development occurs, among nations, under conditions. *But!* There's a principle of convergence, which unifies the process, of the destiny of mankind.

And the best thing to say is, "That's what's going to happen. Enjoy the ride."

That's what our policy has to be.... And that's what our issue is right now. We're going to be going through this week and the next week; and we're on the edge, we're right on the edge, of the extinction of humanity, if things aren't organized the right way.

The Potential of Germany and Russia

And this case of the German case, of the three leading senior officials: On the surface it simply looks like, well, Germany is the only nation which has any integrity as a producer nation in Western Europe. All the others are either dead, or heading for the garbage heap. So therefore, we're not talking about any simplistic thing.

Germany has a technological capability which none of its neighbors do, in terms of productive economy, because you take the economy as a whole. The economy as a whole functions like a unit; so you can't pick out this point and that point and this point. It doesn't work; you've got to look at the economy as a whole. And you've got to find out where the balance lies, which is the difference between collapsing and arising. Germany still has, up until this time, an advantage over all the other nations of Europe in technology, in terms of its productive capabilities. It's the most advanced nation in capabilities in production; in the production of national economy.

So, that is what is being challenged for Russia now by Merkel. Merkel's policy threatens to bring Germany down, as an economy. On the other hand, if Merkel is thrown out—which is the optimal thing—you know, sometimes it's better to throw the garbage away than trying to pick the food out of it. Some people may know that technology. But the point is, if Germany continues to allow the suppression of what its productive potential is in the market; then the German economy will be in trouble, functional trouble. Otherwise, if Germany is allowed, by Germany, to deal with Russia—this is not

CC/Heinz-Josef Lücking

A nuclear power plant in Grohnde, Germany. This plant is noted for having produced the most net electricity per year of any nuclear plant in the world for at least 6 years since its 1984 commissioning.

to make big deals with Russia, but just simple deals with Russia, technology deals—in that case, then you actually do several things. You prevent Europe from becoming what it is now threatening to become—a garbage heap.

So, if you free up the German technological potential in the economy, you suddenly create, what? You open up the development of the economy of Russia. We're not talking about weapons; we're talking about economy, economy in general. In that case, if Germany, which is the dominant economy in Western Europe; every other economy is a piece of shit relative to Germany today; so if that economy is taking over Europe, that driver, that increment, is being injected, the benefit of what Germany can represent injected into Europe generally, what happens? No desire for war.

And the war-makers are threatened, because what happens if Germany integrates, if they try to destroy Germany, or involve Germany in a war, no good result is possible.

And no good for the United States, either. The United States could not survive the effect of a collapse of the Russian economy; because that would be a war economy. And the war system now, which Russia is fully equipped for full-scale warfare, full-scale warfare to take on the United States, too. Do you want that?

Growing Resistance To Obama's War Drive

by Jeffrey Steinberg

The following remarks were made at the June 12 weekly LaRouche PAC webcast, which can be seen in its entirety at the LaRouche PAC website.

June 12—Some things happened today that were quite extraordinary. This really is a moment in which the entire Obama Presidency is standing out there, fully exposed. And I'll get to some of Mr. LaRouche's direct comments on the implications of that in just a moment.

What we do know—and this is just by way of late-breaking news and also by way of some things that you should be on the lookout for over the weekend: President Obama did come this morning to Capitol Hill. Last night, he went to the annual Congressional baseball game—Democrats vs. Republicans—and he showed up basically to harangue Nancy Pelosi to make sure that she was on board for the historic vote today.

The next morning he followed up by going to Capitol Hill to pressure House Democrats. A number of leading Democrats—some of them publicly, and some of them without name attribution—came out of that 40-minute meeting with President Obama, saying they were furious. They said that towards the end of his presentation, he launched into an *ad hominem* diatribe. He basically threatened the Democrats that this was really not any longer about the trade issue, but was about him, and that this was considered in his mind to be a mandate on his Presidency. So, the implications of the overwhelming majority of Democrats voting thumbs-down, of Nancy Pelosi standing up on the floor of the House of Representatives and announcing that she was publicly going to be voting against the President are very profound.

youtube

Rep. Rosa DeLauro (D-Conn), a leader of the Congressional opposition to Fast Track, addresses a rally in April 2015.

Movement vs. Thermonuclear War

What Mr. LaRouche had to say about this, and the strategic implications, and what this says for the period that we're entering into over the immediate days and weeks ahead, is extremely important. And I want to be as precise as possible in terms of what Mr. LaRouche had to say. So, I'm going to read from a very good summary of Mr. LaRouche's words in our discussion this afternoon.

He said the outright rebellion by members of the Democratic Party in Congress against Obama's trade bill today, was not something cobbled together at the last minute, as is being claimed, but, in fact, is a crystallization of a much broader movement of resistance within the institutions against the Obama regime, both inside the United States as well as in Europe. What is happening is a series of events which are energizing the opposition to Obama's attempts to pull off a thermonuclear war.

With the oncoming collapse of the entire trans-Atlantic financial system, Obama, together with his British masters, would be inclined to provoke the occurrence of a thermonuclear war even within the coming three or four weeks. And the stinging defeat he suffered today will tend to *increase* his inclination in that direction even more.

However, in Germany, and now within the United States, Obama is being resisted, and being resisted with great force. And that resistance is growing.

But what is causing this growing resistance? It's that Wall Street is on the chopping block; this bankrupt system cannot continue. The entire trans-Atlantic system is hopelessly bankrupt, and large parts of the world are ready to go in an entirely different direction. The sheer overwhelming numerical strength of their populations [the BRICS nations] makes them quite strong in their power to oppose the will of this dying system.

creative commons
Wall Street insanity, writ large on the floor of the New York Stock Exchange.

However, the danger is that this could lead to chaos. Therefore, we need a program which can handle this collapse of the trans-Atlantic financial system. A showdown in this regard is now underway in the case of Greece; much of Europe is facing imminent crisis, including Spain, Italy, Portugal, and so on. This system cannot be held together for long. Germany is in a relatively stronger position, but what we're seeing right now is a great general breakdown crisis of the entire trans-Atlantic system.

We must take all of these things into consideration simultaneously; and then indicate the nature of what must be done to avoid both of these consequences—the economic breakdown and thermonuclear war. What is needed are policies which will alleviate the factor of panic. We must provide an FDR-style approach, resembling how he defeated the forces of Wall Street in 1932-33. We must have a program which addresses all of the various hardships being experienced by our people: a plan to ameliorate the immediate effects of the crisis, as well as addressing the need for a more general solution to the crisis.

Dump Worthless Debt

What is our problem? The problem is money—worthless money. If we are prepared to cancel these worthless debts, then we can produce a constructive program to allow the people in general to rise in their opportunities of life. To Hell with the filthy rich, the speculators!

We must increase the productivity of the greatest number of people, upgrade their productivity; and we must extend this across the Atlantic as well. Each nation has its own particular problems which need to be solved, but by increasing the general level of productivity overall, we can help each of these countries come together in common interest and for common benefit. The best term to use in this regard is "win-win," as has been specified by the Chinese.

Now, I should add that last night in the course of the discussion with the LaRouche PAC activists—which you can listen to as Matt indicated <u>on this website</u>—Mr. LaRouche called for an American win-win strategy.

So, I think that that's the idea that should be in people's minds as we consider the immediate answer to the question that was asked from our institutional friends, [to] which LaRouche said the following.

LaRouche said the answer to the question, "How do I see the United States economy under the Obama administration?" is simple: It's doomed. What has now become clear is that our President has turned out to be a Republican. No wonder his administration has been such a disaster.

But we can solve this crisis; we just need the constructive policy with which to do it. All this so-called "money" which the banks claim to own is all worthless. It's all gambling money; it doesn't do anything, it's not legitimate. And that takes us back to <u>Glass-Steagall</u>.

What is real productivity, and how can we create real productivity? Just look at Franklin Roosevelt. He didn't believe in the money system; in fact, he talked about the moneychangers in the temple. And he was proud of the fact that they hated him and he hated them right back. He believed in productivity, just as Alexander Hamilton did.

What we have now is negative productivity, quite literally. Wall Street not only has no value, but it has negative value in fact; and Glass-Steagall demonstrates that. Money is only worthwhile if it's used as a weapon to increase productivity—as a means to that end.

Hamilton's Solution to Worthless Debt

How do we replace purely speculative monetary values with real credit which is being put to work for the creation of increases of productivity? Simple. It is all contained within Alexander Hamilton's four Reports to the Congress; and Jason gave us a kind of preliminary map of those four reports during last week's broadcast. And I hope at least some of you out there have taken the time to actually read through them—extraordinarily important—they're founding documents of the American Republic. And when you read them, you will be stunned at how relevant they are today to addressing this question of speculative, worthless money—gambling debt—vs. credit that goes to real productivity.

So, what LaRouche said is, if we look back at what FDR did to overcome the process of accelerating economic depression with the process of increasing economic productivity, we can understand what must be done to reverse the crisis which we face today.

What Roosevelt did to increase the productive powers of the labor force, not only halted the crisis and provided relief to the suffering that was being felt immensely by our people at that time, but succeeded in turning the United States into an economic powerhouse such that the world had never seen before.

This is what came to be the arsenal of democracy. Yes, in the war period, it was turned toward military production, but prior to that, Roosevelt had created such an increase in the productive powers of labor of the overwhelming majority of Americans, that had created the basis for the kind of increase of productivity that is so vitally needed today.

All we need to do is really look at those principles as they've been further advanced and elaborated by Mr. LaRouche; the concept of energy-flux density, for example, is one much more scientifically precise measure of how you define boosts in productivity.

LaRouche concluded that the question which we must address, is how do we do that same thing today? How do we launch a program to restructure our econ-omy at the same time that Obama is going down in defeat? We must set ourselves the task of creating the future; and the key term is "win-win."

The point is, there is a much more profound principle to be addressed, which is not always easy to get across, but which is crucial; the idea of what is mankind. What is the purpose of mankind? How can we fulfill our mission of achieving increasing rates of progress within this galactic system, which we are now only beginning to get a window into, and are only now beginning to get a glimpse of?

Mankind is absolutely distinct from the animal, something which the great Russian scientist Vladimir Vernadsky understood. Animal species may be able to innovate; but they can't create.

And this is what we must understand as our primary consideration when it comes to the task that we now have before us; to face these two simultaneous threats to mankind's existence—economic breakdown and thermonuclear war. And carry out the type of sweeping changes needed in the face of both of these threats in order to insure the continued existence of mankind.

War Danger Is Imminent

Those were Mr. LaRouche's comments. I just want to add that the situation that we're facing, what he referred to earlier in this discussion as a crisis that could play out as early as the next three to four weeks, is that you've got simultaneously, a showdown deadline of June 30 for the Greek debt crisis; which is really the crisis of the entire trans-Atlantic financial system.

And in that same timeframe, President Obama—on behalf of London—is moving to escalate the confrontation against both Russia and China. Russia is the most immediate and obvious target, but China represents the real anchor and the depth of the new win-win paradigm. So, you can't separate the threat to Russia from the intent of Obama and the British to also carry out a major threat to China at the same time.

Right now, what do we have? We have NATO maneuvers going on in the Baltic Sea right off the Russian coast, which are going to be going on throughout the month of June. You have ground maneuvers in Poland; you have the construction of an Aegis ground-based missile defense system right on the Black Sea in Romania. And you've had incursions into the Black Sea by destroyers equipped with Aegis Combat systems, coming into the very edge of Russian coastal waters.

All of these things are going on at the same time

that, just in these past few days, the Prime Minister of Ukraine, Arseniy Yatsenyuk—whom Victoria Nuland fondly refers to as her "Yats"—was in Washington at the same time that Samantha Power was sent to Kiev to really deliver a blood-curdling attack against President Putin of Russia, and to blame the entirety of the Ukraine-Russian crisis on Putin, personally, and on Russia, fully ignoring the fact that Victoria Nuland, Samantha Power—this apparatus—installed a neo-Nazi regime in Kiev, on the basis of an illegal military coup, carried out by these neo-Nazi paramilitaries.

Now, this week, the House of Representatives passed an Amendment [to the Department of Defense Authorization Act of 2015, H.R. 2685], that passed by a unanimous voice-vote, indicating that the U.S. should provide no military assistance to the Azov Brigade, which is explicitly identified in this Congressional resolution as a neo-Nazi organization. The Russian media today took note of this and said, "better late than never. This is exactly what we've been saying since the beginning of the Ukraine crisis."

Now, the Ukrainian government, clearly under instructions from Obama and Newland and now Power, has cut off all military cooperation with Russia, which means that the overflight permission that Russia had had for years, to provide supplies and personnel rotation to Russian peacekeepers in the Transdniestria region—a breakaway region next to Moldova, on the Ukrainian border—has now been cut off.

So, this incident, alone, represents the potential for a new "Sarajevo moment," except the difference between then and now, is that we're facing potential thermonuclear war.

The United States, this week, formally accused Russia of violating the Intermediate-Range Nuclear Force (INF) Treaty, which was signed in 1987, and yet the United States refused to provide any details, whatsoever, of what the so-called violations are. But the U.S. administration announced that it is considering withdrawing from the INF Treaty and resuming the deployment of intermediate-range missiles to Europe, carrying nuclear warheads.

The British government, not surprisingly, has welcomed this offer with open arms, and is considering basing these new intermediate-range advanced, much more modern weapons on British soil. There is an increasing deployment of tactical nuclear weapons into parts of Western Europe, stretching into Eastern Europe.

In other words, the idea of a danger of a hair-trigger

UN photo/Yubi Hoffmann

Samantha Power, Obama's Representative to the United Nations, furthered his war drive with a speech in Kiev on June 11. She is pictured here at the UN in September 2014.

for thermonuclear war, is very real. Fortunately, there are people in Europe, in the United States, who see this madness and want nothing of it.

But the question that Mr. LaRouche posed throughout this past week, is: Will these forces have the courage to take the necessary measures?

[Chancellor Angela] Merkel, in Germany, should be removed from office. The issues are there, with the NSA scandal, and other things. The SPD portion of the coalition government broke with her decisively. Former Chancellor Helmut Schmidt, former Chancellor Gerhard Schröder, current Foreign Minister [Frank-Walter] Steinmeier—have all come out and said that Merkel made a horrible and dangerous mistake, in not inviting Putin to attend the G7 meeting that she hosted several days ago. So, there are splits there.

The events today demonstrate that the Democratic Party is in a state of revolt against Obama. Given the war danger, given the danger of chaos, the real question is: Will *you* make sure, that those people who understand, at least in a limited way, that Obama is an enemy to the future of this country, take the proper steps?

He's committed impeachable crimes. The idea of playing around with nuclear war, is a form of insanity. That, alone, could be a trigger for invoking the 25th Amendment. But that means that *you*'ve got to be on the case. Members of Congress are moving in a certain direction, but left to their own devices, they won't go far enough. The burden is on our shoulders.

Rebuilding the World In the BRICS Era

June 17—On June 13 and 14, eminent representatives of three of the five countries which make up the BRICS (the five are Brazil, Russia, India, China, and South Africa),—and of countries associated with them, were invited to Paris, to speak at an exceptional international conference of the Schiller Institute on the theme: "Rebuilding the World in the BRICS Era."

The aim of this conference, which gathered about 500 people, was to bring to France and to Europe, the winds of progress now blowing over the BRICS and their allies. This will help Europe rise against an international order which has nothing more to offer, other than the return of Empires; the war of all against all; and the systematic looting of populations and public goods.

The conference sharply attacked the Malthusianism spread by the "climate change" swindle, and the UN climate change conference (COP 21) currently being organized in France. That Malthusianism is the mortal enemy of the development of the BRICS and of the rest of the planet.

War, or Peace through Economic Development

Helga Zepp-Larouche, founder and president of the Schiller Institute, keynoted the conference by outlining the perils ahead of us. These are a financial crisis that could rapidly turn into an implosion of the system, as we move towards the final issue of the Greek crisis by the end of June; and the growing threat of war, including nuclear war, against Russia and China. The source for that war drive in the Anglo-American camp is the neo-conservative ideology of the PNAC (Project for a New American Century), which proclaims that no other power should be allowed to rival the global power of the British Empire's Anglo-American relationship.

In that context, Mrs. LaRouche's husband, American political figure and economist Lyndon Larouche, addressed a video message to the conference. In it, he supported the protests of three high-level Gerrman figures: two former German Chancellors, Helmut Schmidt and Gerhard Schroeder, and the current Minister of Foreign Affairs, Frank-Walter Steinmeier,—against Chancellor Merkel's refusal to invite Vladimir Putin to the last G7 summit.

Mrs. LaRouche, however, was optimistic in presenting the BRICS, the New Silk Road of Chinese President Xi Jinping, and the Eurasian Economic Union, as the alternatives to those dangers. She also noted that for at least 25 years, her Institute has been contributing to build those alternatives, by proposing since the time of the fall of the Berlin Wall, an international order of peace through mutual development for the Twenty-First Century,—based on the launching of infrastructure corridors across Eurasia.

Russia, China, and India

The representatives of Russia, China, and India (the only three of the BRICS countries present at the conference, since Brazil and South Africa could not send representatives), gave the conference a sensuous idea of the "polycentric" world, the embryo of the new, more just international economic order that they are fighting for. It is now coming into being at breathtaking speed. The Ambassador of Iran to France, his Excellency Ali Ahani, also sent a message, indicating that the Islamic Republic of Iran is "willing and ready to cooperate with the BRICS countries in order to contribute its aid and cooperation to the solution of regional and world problems."

Russia became Acting President of the BRICS in April, and Mr. Leonid Kadyshev, Minister Councillor of the Russian Embassy in Paris, listed the priorities that the Russian presidency will announce at the upcoming BRICS summit, at Ufa (Russia) on July 9th and 10th.

Before the summit is convened, the New Development Bank (NDB) and the Contingent Reserve Arrangement (CRA), adopted at the Fortaleza summit in 2014, will be launched, since their ratification process is "going well," he reported. A road map will be adopted defining precise investments in infrastructure projects, as well as a new axis of cooperation in areas such as "mining, energy and communications."

Professor Shi Ze of the China Institute of International Studies, then went through the different goals of China's New Silk Road: solving internal economic imbalances between its eastern and western regions, and improving its foreign trade with its western neighbors (Central Asia, India and Russia). These can contribute to meeting China's great energy needs for its development. But the same "One Belt, One Road," strategy, is also China's contribution to the world in the Confucian tradition: to create via "the development of the Eurasian continent;.. a new locomotive for growth in the world," and to "reinforce peace and worldwide security."

An important contribution followed from Indian former Ambassador Viswanathan, Senior Fellow at the Observer Research Foundation, who is the coordinator of all its activities connected with the BRICS. In view of the fact that the BRICS represent 25% of the world's GDP, but only 11% of the voting rights in the IMF, he denounced the "completely anachronistic character... of the IMF, the World Bank and the Security Council of the UN."

Rather than only aspiring for a better order, the BRICS have now become an active force, setting the international agenda so as to bring that order into being. Two examples are the creation of the NDB, and that of the Contingent Reserve Arrangement (CRA), which Mr. Viswanathan pointed to as the first world institutions created in 200 years without the participation of the West.

The future is "looks bright" for the BRICS, he said, adding however that "the BRICS is work in progress and not a finished product."

The two days of intense discussions hundreds of Frenchmen and delegations involved from Germany, Denmark, Sweden, Spain, Italy, Australia, Poland, Rumania, Russia, China, and Peru, among other countries. Participants understood that they were not attending any ordinary conference, but rather were participating in an ongoing international fight for their survival and that of the human race. Many decided to engage actively, and become the authors of their own destiny.

The full program is appended here.

Rebuilding the World in the Brics Era

International Conference of the Schiller Institute
Paris, 13-14 June 2015

Saturday June 13

The speakers who hold government or institutional positions, and some of whom have participated in the negotiation process leading to the BRICS, will all speak in a personal capacity.

KEYNOTE

Helga Zepp-LaRouche,
Chairwoman of the Schiller Institute

PANEL I:

The New Silk Road and the BRICS: A New Paradigm for Civilization

Moderator: **Christine Bierre**, journalist, Paris
- **Leonid Kadyshev**, Minister Councillor of the Russian Embassy in France.
- **Prof. Shi Ze**, Senior Research Fellow and Director of International Strategic Studies on Energy of the China Institute of International Studies (CIIS), a think-tank of the Foreign Ministry, Beijing.
- **H.E. Ambassador H.H.S. Viswanathan**, Distinguished Fellow, Observer Research Foundation. Coordinator of all activies connected with BRICS and IBSA (India, Brazil, South Africa, New Delhi).
- **H.E. Ali Ahani**, Ambassador of Iran in France.

PANEL II

Eradicating the Geopolitics of War by Pursuing the Common Aims of Mankind

Moderator: **Elke Fimmen**, Schiller Institute, Germany
- **Denys Pluvinage**, consultant to the French-Russian Dialogue, Paris.

- **Jean-François Di Meglio**, President ASIA Centre, Paris.
- **Jayshree Sengupta**, Economist, observer Research Foundation, New Delhi, India.
- **Colonel (ret.) Alain Corvez**, International Strategy Consultant. Former International Relations Consultant of the Defense and Interior Ministries, Paris.
- **Stélios Kouloglou**, Journalist, Writer, and Member of European Parliament, Syriza, Greece.

PANEL III

Great Infrastructure Projects Are the Only Real Alternative

These experts have all been personally involved in the design, feasibility studies and development of international infrastructure programs.
Moderator: **Rainer Apel**, *Executive Intelligence Review*, Wiesbaden.
- **Christine Bierre**, Journalist, Paris.
- **Jean-Pierre Gérard**, Economist, Entrepreneur, former member of the Economic Council of the Bank of France, Paris.
- **Hussein Askary**, Middle East Director of the Schiller Institute, Stockholm.
- **Prof. Safieeldin Mohamed Metwally**, The National Center for Desert Research, Ciaro, Egypt.
- **Acheikh Ibn-Oumar**, former Foreign Minister of Chad, Reims.

Musical Evening

Sunday June 14

Introductory Remarks

Jacques Cheminade,
President of Solidarité et Progrès, Paris.

PANEL IV

Public Credit and Debt Cancellation, The Political Challenge for Europe

The speakers are aware that European nations must join the BRICS dynamic, bringing with them the best of their respective cultures and historical achievements to expand the scope. The crucial issue is to put the end to monetarism and establish a public credit system both nationally and internationally to finance great infrastructure projects.
Moderator: **Karel Vereycken**, Journalist, Paris.
- **Karel Vereycken**, Journalist, Paris.
- **Dean Andromidas**, *Executive Intelligence Review*, Wiesbaden.
- **Diogène Senny**, Secretary General of the Pan-African League-UMOJA, Toulouse.
- **Prof. Mohamed Ali Ibrahim**, Dean of the Transport and Logistics Institute, Chairman of the Arab League Academy of Science and Technology, Port Said, Egypt.

Messages to the Conference

PANEL V

A New Scientific and Cultural Renaissance is the Key to Our Future

Countering the hypocrisy and the unrealistic vision of the UN climate conference (COP 21) in Paris, the speakers will develop the real reasons for climate change and how human society has to master the dynamics involved for their mutual benefit, starting from an overall solar and galactic perspective.
Moderator: **Odile Mojon**, Schiller Institute, Paris.
- **Maëlle Mercier**, Schiller Institute, Paris.
- **Benjamin Deniston**, LaRouche PAC Scientific Research Team, Washington.
- **Prof. François Gervais**, Professor Emeritus of the François Rabelais University, Tours, Critical Rapporteur to the IPCC-ARS5 (International Panel on Climate Change), Tours.
- **Prof. Carl-Otto Weiss**, Advisor to the European Institute for Climate and Energy; Former President of the National Metrology Institute of Germany, Braunschweig.

CONCLUDING REMARKS

Creating a New Renaissance

- **Helga Zepp-LaRouche,** Chairwoman of the Schiller Institute

Rebuilding the World In the BRICS Era

by Helga Zepp-LaRouche

Helga Zepp-LaRouche

Christopher Lewis

June 13—Thank you, and I welcome you. I would like to preface my actual speech with a short report about what Mr. La-Rouche had to say yesterday, because yesterday we had extremely important breaking developments. President Obama went to the Congress and tried to really threaten the Democratic Party members of the Congress, telling them that they absolutely had to vote for the Fast Track Authority, as it's now called: that this was not about the free trade pact (TPP), but it was about him.

Reports were that when this 40-minute session was over, members of Congress came out completely furious, and then voted with an overwhelming majority *against* this TPP proposition, which is really a major defeat, one more of the many defeats of Obama in the recent period. Mr. LaRouche commented, that this is a reflection not of a last-minute opposition, but this is a process of rebellion going on in the last period on both sides of the Atlantic. And it reflects much more an awareness by important factions, that we are in the danger of immediate nuclear war.

So, he said that that means for the next period, you have to expect even an increase in the inclination of the Obama Administration to push the confrontation, but that the real reason has to be addressed, and that is that

Wall Street is on the chopping block, that the entire trans-Atlantic financial system is hopelessly bankrupt, and that the only hope is in the existence of a bloc of nations who are numerically much stronger. However, he said that what has to be also avoided, is the plunge of the world into chaos. And that therefore, we need a program which immediately addresses the situation, because you have the impending blowout of the Greek debt, which would have immediate consequences for Spain and Italy, and that even if Germany is in a relatively stronger position, we're looking at the breakdown of the entire trans-Atlantic financial system.

Therefore, the kinds of measures which have to be taken, are like what Franklin D. Roosevelt did in the period from '33 to '39, and that is what we have to concentrate on. I think that is something which the deliberations of this conference must deal with.

Because this is not an academic conference. This is an actual effort to intervene in a moment, when it is very clear that the leading institutions of the G7, for example, which just met in their summit, have absolutely failed to address these existential dangers for civilization.

Now I will come back to these optimistic solutions,

FIGURE 1

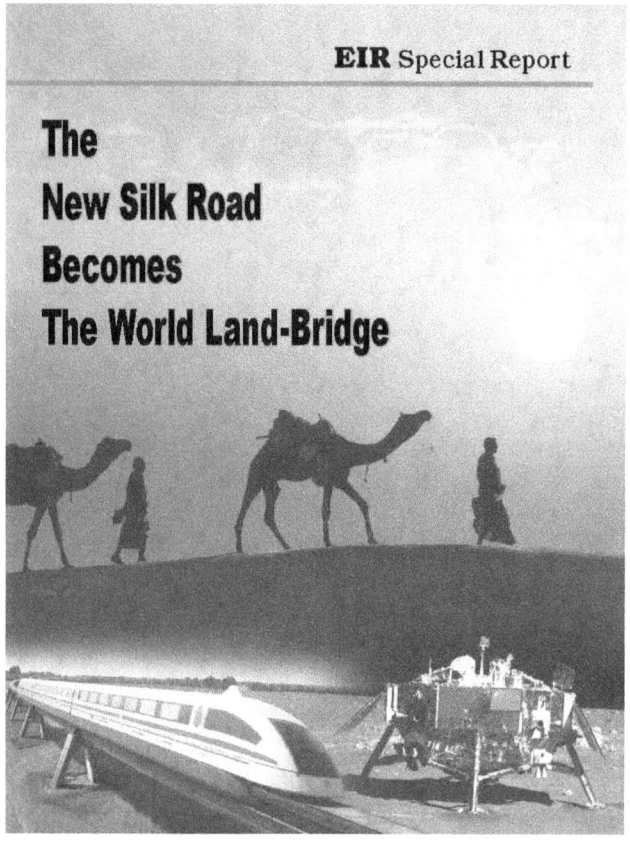

The New Silk Road Becomes The World Land-Bridge

but let me tell you: Mankind has never been at such a dangerous moment.

Beautiful Options

In the beginning, I want to express my conviction that I think it is absolutely possible to save civilization, and realize the very beautiful options and alternatives which will be the subject of this discussion. If we do our job right—and obviously it will not only depend on us, but our subjective intervention, I think, will be the margin of difference as to whether mankind goes into annihilation, or into a new era of civilization—we could have, very soon, a completely different world.

And I think it's important to start with the vision of where we want to go, because we could have a completely different relationship among nations, not focussed on geopolitical confrontation, not focusing on so-called narrow or national interests vs. the national interests of some other country, but where we would be united for the common aims of mankind, such that we could have a new world economic order, which would give justice to every nation on this planet, combined

with a Classical Renaissance of culture, which, in my view, is equally urgent, if you look at the degeneracy of the Western culture at this point.

But that can only be realized if we succeed in realizing the task which we set out for ourselves quite some while ago, namely that we get the European nations, and the United States, in a cooperative mode with the BRICS nations, and the win-win policy of President Xi Jinping of China.

Now, this is the program **Figure 1**, a blueprint for the next 50 years. Maybe, if you look at the speed of developments in China, it will take only 20 years, but it could also be the next 100 years. It is really the key. This program of building a World Land-Bridge, uniting all the nations on the planet in a common development strategy, is really the way in which to overcome all problems.

•The war danger—because it would represent a peace strategy for the Twenty-first Century;

•The underdevelopment and hunger of billions of people—because it would provide development and production for all of them;

•It would eliminate, or help to eliminate, the drug trade, and it would especially give hope for the future, and therefore overcome the decadence of the mind.

However, this shift has to occur very, very suddenly. Because it's very urgent.

G7 Insanity

If you look at the results of the recent G7 summit, well, you have a situation where unfortunately Chancellor Merkel, pushed by Obama, Cameron, and Canada, excluded President Putin for the second time, and that action of Mrs. Merkel created the forum for Obama's very provocative attacks at the end of the Summit.

Now, given the fact that the G7 only represent about 10% of the world's population, I find it quite an enormity that they decided to implement a so-called decarbonization of the world economy by the year 2100. Who authorizes 10% of the world population to define the program of the entire world for 90 years from now?

Mrs. Merkel, if history remembers her, will probably go into history for her very infamous exit from nuclear energy, and the sole reliance on renewable energies. Decarbonization would mean only having solar and wind—no fossil fuel energy resources—and since they are also against nuclear energy in Germany, well, it basically would mean implementing the program of

Zoologist and advocate for population reduction Sir David Attenborough.

Mr. Schellnhuber, who is the head of the VDGU in Germany, an advisory institution, but also a CBE, Commander of the British Empire. He has developed this program of the transformation of the global economy which would be decarbonization of the world economy, and if we realize that there is a direct correlation between the energy flux density in the production process, and the number of people who can be supported with that energy flux density, you have to come to the conclusion that the approximate number of people who could be maintained is about 1 billion people.

Then there was this very ominous meeting between President Obama and Sir David Attenborough. Sir David Attenborough is the key advisor for environmental and energy questions to the British Crown. He was flown in by Obama shortly before the G7 summit, and basically it was not made public what they discussed, but we know what Attenborough has said in the past: namely, that mankind is a plague. That we should purge it massively by at least half; so you can assume that what went into this summit on the side of Obama, was the British advice on how to reduce population.

Now, fortunately, there are three important German personalities who intervened shortly before the G7 Summit, saying that President Putin *should* be invited. They were, very importantly, the current Foreign Minister Frank-Walter Steinmeier; and the former Chancellors Gerhard Schröder and Helmut Schmidt; and Helmut Schmidt, in particular, said not only that Russia should be invited to the G7 summit, but China and India as well. And Schmidt, who is 95 years old—it seems to be the quality of older people that they are often more

courageous in speaking the truth, than younger people—had warned of World War III many, many times before.

So, you can be assured that these people—Steinmeier in that sense really being on a completely different track than Merkel— know the warnings which military experts in the recent period have expressed: Namely, that we are today in a situation that is more dangerous than at the height of the Cold War. And the height of the Cold War was the Cuban Missile crisis.

Now during the Cuban Missile crisis, you had, despite the extremely adversarial relations, communications between President Kennedy and Khrushchov, and they were able to defuse the crisis at the very last moment.

That is not the case between President Obama and President Putin. It has been noted by many military experts that the biggest danger, or one of the biggest dangers, is that there is no communication between the United States and Russia, in particular.

A Cuban Missile Crisis in Reverse

How did we get to this crisis?

This has been the result of a long-term buildup, which really started with the decision of the neo-cons in 1997 to go for the policy of the PNAC, the Project for a New American Century. This was the idea that, especially when the Soviet Union disintegrated, between '89 and '91, no country could refuse to be part of an Empire run by the Anglo-Americans, based on the special relationship between Great Britain and the United States. And it was explicitly noted that the goal was to maintain a U.S. global pre-eminence precluding the rise of a power, or a group of nations, who could challenge the power of the United States. And it is that concept which still exists. It was only briefly interrupted halfway into the Clinton period. It was fully carried on by Bush Sr. and Bush Jr.—two administrations—and now by six and a half years of Obama.

So what this policy meant is that immediately following the collapse of the Soviet Union, the neo-cons went into policies of regime change, through a variety of measures—color revolution, paying NGOs with the aim of toppling the democratically elected government, with policies of sanctions—we see it in the case of Russia, where the exclusive aim of these sanctions is to cause so much uproar inside Russia, that you would have a Maidan phenomenon in Moscow, and get rid of Putin.

These policies included the NATO and EU expan-

President Kennedy consults the military at the time of the Cuban Missile crisis—but he was also able to talk with the Kremlin.

sion to the borders of Russia, whereas, according to Jack F. Matlock, who was the American Ambassador in Moscow during the time of the collapse of the Soviet Union, promises were given that this would never happen. These promises were never kept. And it means troop and military equipment forward-positioning at the Russian borders.

And now, very recently, you have the extremely flimsy accusation that Russia has violated the INF treaty, and that this could be related to an alleged test-launch of a sea-based cruise missile from a launcher on land, which, if it ever happened, or something similar, would have been an extremely minor technical thing,—but, as I said, it's not even proven. The Russian side has maintained very clearly that there is no proof, and Deputy Defense Minister Antonov basically has said the U.S. is ramping up these allegations against Russia, to justify their own military plans to return the U.S. short- and medium- range missiles to Europe and other regions.

When Obama came into office, he had promised that he would reduce nuclear weapons, and eventually get rid of them, but now, for him to put nuclear weapons back into Great Britain—which already has been accepted, in the person of Cameron—and other places, is really a push for nuclear war. Some people think it would be nuclear war in Europe, but by the logic of nuclear war, it would not be just for Europe. It would be a generalized global thermonuclear war, which nobody would survive.

General Leonid Ivashov, who is right now the head of the Academy of Geopolitics, said this is a Cuban missile crisis in reverse. And it is the acting-out of the Cheney-Wolfowitz doctrine of a unipolar world.

Now the Obama Administration has admitted that it is considering an option of leaving the INF Treaty, deploying so-called counterforce IRBMs (intermediate-range ballistic missiles) to Europe, or even a countervailing strike capability involving the possibility of a pre-emptive nuclear attack on targets inside of Russia.

Also, the transformation of the military doctrine during the last period—Prompt Global Strike, and the U.S. Ballistic Missile System are *de facto* first strike doctrines. And if you remember what President Putin said when he announced the upgrade of the Russian military doctrine over the Christmas period,—he said there may come a point where Russia feels compelled to use nuclear weapons to avoid this danger. That should show you why we are really in mortal danger, and absolutely must act.

The NATO website presently lists 71 maneuvers and events between April and November, all close to the Russian border, in the Baltics, the Baltic Sea and the Black Sea. And Poroshenko just announced that he is ending all military cooperation with Russia, which blocks the supply of Russian troops in Transdniestria, Moldova, and this, on the surface, could be a repeat of the events of Georgia in 2008, but it could also be a pretext used for actions against Russia.

Russia is intensifying its strategic ties with China and India, and Russia and China are drilling their airborne amphibious troops in the Far East, in a maneuver called Joint Sea 2015.

In light of the fact that the pretext for all of this escalation against Russia is the Ukraine situation, supposedly the Crimea issue,—it should be absolutely noted that what triggered this event was, on the one side, the fascist coup in Kiev on February 18-22, 2014; and before that, the effort to incorporate Ukraine into the EU through the EU Association Agreement; and even before that, as Helmut Schmidt said, and I fully agree: the real Ukraine crisis started with the Maastricht Treaty, because this is where the idea of having an eastward expansion of the EU really started.

So what happened therefore at the G7 meeting, you could only call a suicidal delirium on the side of Germany, France, Italy, and other nations. The only chance is that the opposition of Steinmeier, Schmidt, and Schröder has to be escalated. Merkel, in my view, should be replaced, because she is violating her oath of office—to protect the German people against perils—and because of her scandalous behavior in the NSA-BND affair, which violates the rights of all German people, and not only the German people. Because, as you know, the BND-NSA collaboration spied against France, against Belgium, Austria, even Germany's own industry,—and Merkel obviously doesn't know that the German economy, without cooperation with Russia and the BRICS, does not function.

UNHCR/F. Malavolta

These refugees from Africa and the Middle East were rescued in the Mediterranean in April 2015. Here they're shown arriving in Palermo, Italy.

Now, Russia is part of Europe, and the sanctions designed to harm Russia are really extremely stupid. Because they not only hurt Russia, which obviously is suffering from them, but, for example, in the first quarter of this year, German machine tool exports to Russia collapsed by 28%, and German industry is extremely furious that the U.S. exports to Russia in the same period, increased by 17%.

Basically, there is not only stagnation in the economy of Europe, but there is right now nothing to protect all of Europe from disintegration, especially in light of the pending explosion of the Greek situation, which seems clearly to be coming to a head.

So Merkel should be either forced out, or she should be completely reined in, subdued, by forces in Germany from industry, the military, and a larger faction in the SPD, represented by these three individuals. But we should also be aware that the United States has long been running on this geopolitical idea, of preventing collaboration between Germany and Russia. I think that

what needs to be done—and it is not just the task of Germany—but all of Europe has to make sure that the sanctions are ended right away. And it's very easy. All we have to say is, we are starting to trade with Russia again, and that would be the very first step to get back to normality.

A Policy of Genocide

But the declaration of decarbonization and economic warfare against Russia are not the only terrible evils which were agreed upon at the G7 summit. They decided on a hard line against Greece, an austerity policy to the total advantage of the too-big-to-fail banks, and one should note that 97% of all the so-called rescue packages, really went back to the banks. And what is being imposed on Greece is the kind of debt dungeon, or debt corset, in the tradition of Versailles and Brüning. And Jean Ziegler, who's a prominent Swiss activist and UN representative, basically said the modern slaveholders are sitting in the upper floors of the banks and multinationals. And he called the present system of globalization "cannibalistic," and that is absolutely true.

Your average Eurocentrist will say: Oh, Mr. Ziegler is too radical. But if you think about it, is it not true? What is the difference between the ships of the slave traders and plantation owners of the Confederacy,

The toll of the Ebola "pestilence" in Sierra Leone in September 2014.

where thousands of people drowned or died of hunger and thirst, and the refugee crisis in the Mediterranean, where many thousands of people, almost every week, are risking their lives and that of their children, having a 50% chance of not making it, running away from wars in the Middle East, starvation, and epidemics in Africa, and terrorism?

The EU policy on refugees, for me, reflects the total moral bankruptcy of that institution. Because the EU is only serving the interests of the too-big-to-fail banks and the IMF, which are run by the interests which basically have turned the whole developing sector into a plantation. You think about the land grab, speculation on scarcity of water, blocking water management projects with the purpose of having high water prices, to speculate in bottled water, controlling the food chain. Jean Ziegler said that every child who dies of hunger, is murdered. And I agree. Because it would be so easy to solve it. It would take half a year, and you could eliminate that from happening.

A few days ago, on the plane, I watched the movie "Twelve Years a Slave," which is a remarkable movie. I normally don't encourage people to watch movies, but this one is very advisable. Because it captures the mentality of the slaveholders which is today alive and kicking in the U.S. pro-British tendency.

Behind this unipolar world outlook, is, in reality, the mentality of plantation owners and slaveholders in the modern form. Granted, the CEOs of too-big-to-fail banks and the EU bureaucrats probably don't have the perverse lust which is portrayed in this movie, where you can really say that the sadism and absolutely disgusting mentality goes to the borders of what human beings should be able to do. But nevertheless, they are the masterminds, behind the desks; they are the perpetrators at the desks; they speculate with CO_2 certificates, and they couldn't care less about the consequences of their policies. As long as they have profit, what happens to the people as a result, leaves them completely indifferent.

This brings us back to Mr. Attenborough, who said that we human beings are the plague on the Earth, and that we have to fight the explosion in human numbers. He is associated with the so-called Optimum Population Trust (now called Population Matters), which basically says that the present number of people on the planet, has to be reduced before the end of the century to half—that would be 3.5 billion. One in every two people? You have to take it very personally.

Friedrich Schiller, in the very beautiful essay "The Legislation of Lycurgus and Solon," portrayed Sparta as the oligarchical model, in which he said that the oligarchical model permits the elimination of the so-called helots. They can be killed off if there are too many. Bertrand Russell, in his book *The Impact of Science on Society*, wrote:

> 'Bad times, you may say, are exceptional, and can be dealt with by exceptional methods. This has been more or less true during the honeymoon period of industrialism, but it will not remain true, unless the increase of population can be enormously diminished. At present the population of the world is increasing at about 58,000 per diem. War, so far, has had no very great effect on this increase, which continued through each of the world wars... War has hitherto been disappointing in this respect... but perhaps bacteriological war may prove more effective. If a Black Death could spread throughout the world once in every generation, survivors could procreate freely without making the world too full. The

state of affairs might be unpleasant, but what of it? Really high-minded people are indifferent to happiness, especially of other people.

In his *Prospects of Industrial Civilization*, Russell wrote:

> The white population of the world will soon cease to increase. The Asiatic races will be longer, and the negroes still longer, before their birth rate falls sufficiently to make their numbers stable without help of war and pestilence... Until that happens, the benefits aimed at by socialism can only be partially realized, and the less prolific races will have to defend themselves against the more prolific by methods which are disgusting even if they are necessary.

With that mindset, a splendid little war—as the British always used to call it—seems to be just the right thing, even a splendid little nuclear war. It may be disgusting, but necessary.

The Promise of the Silk Road

Now, fortunately, there is an alternative.

Since about two years ago, when President Xi Jinping announced the New Silk Road and the maritime Silk Road, and especially since the Fortaleza Summit in July 2014, there has been a completely different economic system. The BRICS have made among themselves an enormous number of deals: areas of cooperation, involving infrastructure, science and technology, nuclear energy, space development, worth several trillions of euros, dollars, and so forth.

From the standpoint of European habits of the last couple of years, these countries have done so with an unbelievable speed, and other organizations have coalesced around the BRICS. All of Latin America, most of ASEAN, parts of Africa, and even Europe. With Chinese help, they are now building a second Panama Canal in Nicaragua. The Chinese are planning to build a trans-continental railway between Brazil and Peru. This plan was concluded at the recent visit of Prime Minister Li Keqiang in Latin America. And they are also building four tunnels between Chile and Argen-

Xinhua/Ding Lin

Chinese Premier Li Keqiang in Santiago, Chile with Chilean President Michelle Bachelet, on May 25, 2015.

tina, all with direct Chinese investment.

But beyond that, the BRICS have created a completely parallel financial system: the New Development Bank, with initial capital of $100 billion; the Currency Reserve Arrangement, which is a pool to defend participating countries against speculation; the AIIB, the Asian Infrastructure Investment Bank, where, contrary to the wishes of the Obama Administration, 58 nations rushed to be founding members, including France, Germany, Italy, and Scandinavia. The Shanghai Cooperation Organization has a new bank; so does SAARC, the South Asian Association for Regional Cooperation. There is a New Silk Road development fund, and a Maritime Silk Road Fund. And they all have the explicit aim of filling the vacuum that has been left by the IMF and the World Bank, who only spend $60 billion a year for infrastructure investment, and therefore, these banks have now engaged in an effort to invest in huge infrastructure development programs all over the developing sector.

Now the main impetus of this clearly came from the Chinese President Xi Jinping, but there is also an extremely strong strategic partnership between Russia and China. The New Silk Road, and "One Road, One Belt" policy has, in the recent period, completely integrated with the Eurasian Economic Union of Russia, Belarus, Kazakstan, Armenia, and Kyrgyzstan. There is an extremely close strategic cooperation between Russia and India, and at a recent visit of President Putin

Press Trust of India

Indian Prime Minister Narendra Modi (right) and Russian President Vladimir Putin at their press conference in New Delhi, December 11, 2014.

to India, President Modi said that India and Russia are united by the strongest strategic partnership in respect to security in the past, and it will be like that for the indefinite future.

Also, between India and China, the strategic partnership has been strengthened, and territorial and other conflicts have been put on ice. At the visit of Li Keqiang to Brazil, a couple of weeks ago, he was able to completely reverse a strategic attack on Brazil by Wall Street, and stop the destabilization efforts against Dilma Rousseff.

So, there is right now emerging, a completely different model of relations among nations, based on completely different principles. Not so completely different, because they used to be the property of the United Nations, before this imperial policy took over. Like non-interference, respect for the different social models, mutual economic benefit, a "win-win" policy.

Obviously this new model of economy has an enormous attractiveness, and it has led to an eruption of optimism. Projects which have been on the shelf in many countries, have been taken off and are now being realized.

The Chinese economic miracle has become contagious. China, since the reforms of Deng Xiaoping, and especially in the last 30 years, has developed at breathtaking speed, and was able to do what the industrial-

ized nations needed 150 to 200 years to do. China, contrary to the coverage in the Western media, has the best human rights record in the world, because they have transformed 800 million people from extreme poverty, into a very decent living standard. And what is a greater human rights violation than poverty?

Now, with the New Silk Road, China is also intending to upgrade the not-yet-developed parts in its interior region, and upgrade the living standard of the rural population. It has announced that it wants to double the GDP from 2010 to 2020. Now that is a remarkable goal, and it is believable if you look at what happened in the last 30 years.

The Realization of Our Vision

Now, for us in the Schiller Institute, the New Silk Road is a realization of a vision which we started to develop 25 years ago. At the time of the Fall of the Wall, we proposed to unite the region between Paris, Berlin, and Vienna into the so-called Productive Triangle, because the Wall was no longer there. And when the Soviet Union collapsed in '91, (**Figure 2**) we extended that Productive Triangle into the so-called Eurasian Land-Bridge. This was the idea of uniting the industrial and population centers of Europe with those of Asia, through so-called Development Infrastructure Corridors, but it was not only meant as an economic program. It was deliberately meant as a peace-order for the Twenty-First Century.

The Eurasian Land-Bridge was the idea of having a higher order of reason, where historic conflicts, tensions, ethnic tensions, and so forth—wounds of the battles of the past—would be overcome because there would be a mutual benefit for everybody to participate in this program. It was really, even if we didn't call it that, a "win-win" policy.

Now, naturally, it did not get realized, because of the reason I just said—the Project for a New American Century, the efforts by Bush Sr., Margaret Thatcher, and Mitterrand, to force Germany at the time of the German unification, to give up the D-mark for the euro. And the Maastricht Treaty. But, up to '89, it was the so-called best-kept secret of NATO that Germany was still

FIGURE 2

Eurasia: Main Routes and Selected Secondary Routes of the Eurasian Land-Bridge

an occupied country,—and the Maastricht Treaty would insure that Germany would remain an occupied country, by containment, by putting Germany into the straitjacket of the Stability Pact, the debt brake,—and it was clear to us that the euro could not function, because it was not designed to be an economic program. It was a geopolitical attack on Germany.

At that time, we conducted hundreds of conferences and seminars on five continents, and in '96, at a conference in Beijing on the Eurasian Land-Bridge, that program was *de facto* put on the agenda by the Chinese government to be the strategic perspective for the year 2010. And naturally that got interrupted by the Asia crisis in '97, and the Russian state bankruptcy in '98.

Therefore, we were overjoyed, but not fundamentally surprised, when Xi Jinping announced the New Silk Road.

Now, for about two years, the mainstream media has completely ignored the fact that a parallel economic system is developing, or they slandered it by giving

Putin a bad name, or Xi Jinping. But for the last four weeks, you have a flood of articles. As in *Time* magazine: "New Silk Road Could Change Global Economics Forever;" "Great Infrastructure Projects in History—This is a great game over the control of Eurasia, It could lead to a New Cold War. The outcome is uncertain."

Deutschlandfunk also has had coverage of the New Silk Road.

Most of these articles are all of a sudden saying, there is a completely new system, but you know, it is still really geopolitics. And they completely miss the point that this is explicitly a way to *overcome* geopolitics by inviting everybody in the whole world to participate.

They also say, China must have a secret agenda. They want to take over the world. They want to replace American imperialism with Chinese imperialism, and it is very clear that the journalists and politicians of the trans-Atlantic region, have an extremely hard time

Athens' Solon (left) versus Sparta's Lycurgus (right) represent two contrasting models of the state and nature of man.

imagining that there could be governments which are devoted to the common good. Because you have not had such governments for such a long time, that it's almost a distant memory. It reminds me of Hegel's words, when he wrote that if a world-historical individual has a valet (a butler), that the valet, who sees the world-historical individual always in only his underwear, cannot imagine that he's a world-historical individual. But he says, this is not because the world-historical individual is not a world-historical individual, but because the valet is a valet.

Now, the key to understanding the real motives of China is Confucius.

From Confucius to Schiller: The Beautiful Soul

Confucius has, along with Mencius, influenced Chinese philosophy, actually the Chinese state philosophy, for about 2,500 years. That philosophy has an image of man that man is good by nature. The key notions of the Chinese philosophy are *ren*, which is the idea corresponding to *agapē*—love, charity in the Christian tradition; and the idea of *li*, meaning principle, which is the idea that if each person and each thing develops in the best possible way, you have harmony in society. This corresponds to the idea of Nicolas of Cusa, that if each microcosm develops in the best way, you have concordance in the macrocosm; or the idea of the *monad* of

Leibniz, that if each develops his fullest potential, you have harmony.

Now, the idea of harmony is very central to Confucian philosophy. It is not an aesthetic relationship, but a contrapuntal development of mutual forward development: If all microcosms develop in the optimal way, you have harmony in the macrocosm.

There's also the idea that there is such a thing as the Mandate of Heaven: that there must be harmony between nature and man, and this comes originally from the idea of God's will of the Western Zhou dynasty, from 1046-771 B.C., which said that there must be harmony between the heavens and man, and that they are closely related.

This concept, by the way, exists in all great religions and philosophies: You have the same idea of cosmology in India, coming from the Hindu tradition. You have it in the form of natural law in the European tradition. And it is really what we have to come to as humanity, if we are to overcome the present level of thinking.

Harmony without uniformity is what Confucius writes about in his *Analects*. Unity in diversity is the idea as expressed by Nicolas of Cusa. In the *Book of Rites*, which is the preface to the *Great Learning* of Confucius,—it's attributed to him,—he says:

> The ancients, wishing that all men under Heaven keep their inborn luminous virtue unobscured, first had to govern the nation well; wishing to govern the nation well, they first established harmony in their household; wishing to establish harmony within their households, they first cultivated themselves; wishing to cultivate themselves, they first set their minds in the right; wishing to set their minds in the right, they first developed sincerity of thought; wishing to have sincerity of thought, they first extended their knowledge to the utmost. The extension of knowledge to the utmost lies in fully apprehending the principle of things.

Now, harmony in society and among nations is based on an understanding of the principles of things. This is the same idea Friedrich Schiller has in the *Aesthetical Letters*, that only scientists and Classical artists understand the truth. Xi Jinping, in his book *Governance of China*, which is a collection of 71 of his speeches, 2013-14, reflects this Confucian spirit. He quotes an ancient Chinese saying:

> Learning is the bow, while competence is the arrow. You should regard learning as the top priority, a responsibility, a moral support and a lifestyle. You should establish a conviction that dreams start from learning.

Xi said:

> This is what Confucius meant when he said 'if you can in one day renovate yourself, do so from day to day.' Yes, let there be daily renovation. Life never favors those who follow the beaten track, and are satisfied with the status quo, and it never waits for the unambitious and those who sit idle and enjoy the fruits of others' work.

This is what Lyndon LaRouche says to us every day: that we cannot do today what we did yesterday, and that each day we have to be creative and innovative. Xi Jinping quotes Victor Hugo, who said, "Things created are insignificant, when compared with things to be created."

China has been able to progress step by step over centuries, thanks to the tenacity of generations, one after another, and to the nation's spirit of constant self-improvement through hard work. "Innovation-based economy" is what China is aiming at and already realizing: not to have "Made in China," but "Created in

China's work on the frontiers of science includes thermonuclear fusion power. Here, China's EAST fusion reactor, the first fully superconducting Tokamak in the world.

China." Xi Jinping has demanded breakthroughs in basic scientific fields such as the structure of matter, the evolution of the universe, the origin of life, and the nature of consciousness.

Where does the new road lie? It lies in scientific and technological innovation, the acceleration of innovation-driven growth, and he also said that they are proud to have the most scientists and engineers in the world.

But I was most impressed when I found this quote by Xi Jinping:

> Like the spring drizzle falling without a sound, we should disseminate the core socialist values in a gentle and lively way, by making use of all kinds of cultural forms. We should inform the people by means of fine literary works, and artistic images: What is the true, the good, and the beautiful? What is the false, the evil, and the ugly? And what should be praised and encouraged, and what should be opposed and repudiated?

I wish we would have politicians in Europe and in the United States who call for the "implementation of the true, the good, and the beautiful." Because the idea, that there is a coherence between those—the true, the good, and the beautiful—was the idea of the ancient Greek Classics; that there is a knowable truth; that man is good; that when he is a truth-seeking individual, what he then discovers is beauty, as well as that the process of discovery is beautiful. The idea of "the true, the good, and the beautiful," is the essence of the German Classical period, and Friedrich Schiller said, "Art is only art if it is beautiful, because only then does it elevate the human soul."

Now, by that definition, most of what is being produced today, does not qualify as art, because it's not beautiful. Because the idea of beauty is an idea derived from reason, not from sensuous experience. Schiller is emphatic on that: that you do not define beauty by your opinion, your likings, but that there is an idea of beauty associated with reason, although at the same time, it appeals to the senses; and that through aesthetical education, beauty becomes the synonym for the happy reconciliation between reason and sensuousness: That in beauty, things harmonize.

For Friedrich Schiller, the highest idea of man was the beautiful soul for whom freedom and necessity, passion and duty, are one. But also, the analogy between beauty and freedom is pretty obvious, because both are not determined from the outside, but from the inside. The greatest idea of self-determination reflects itself from certain characteristics of nature, and that we call "beauty."

But beauty is also, according to Schiller, a necessary condition of mankind. The state is merely the means; the goal is humanity alone. The ideal of the state presumes, therefore, the ideal of mankind, and the idea of mankind is based on the laws of the beautiful. Schiller in 1789 writes to his friend Körner:

What is the life of man if you take away what art gives to him? An eternally discovered sight of

The Poet of Freedom, Friedrich Schiller

destruction. Because if you take out of our life what serves beauty, the only thing remaining is need, and what is need, other than protection against the always-threatening demise?

Schiller, with that, most convincingly argues against the state whose only purpose is the maintenance of power, which is what the state is today! The politicians have no interest in beauty or the perfection of their people, but in keeping their job, in keeping their position. But only when the beautiful has become the purpose of the life of the people and nations, rather than the necessity of organizing everything for protection against permanently-threatening doom, do you have humanity. The condition of the West, especially in the United States after September 11 should really be looked at from the standpoint of the soon-to-be-published 28 pages, revealing who really financed the terrorist attack; and the DIA documents pertaining to what really happened in the Benghazi attack. But the war against terrorism has become a hydra, where life has become quite miserable by being reduced to only protecting people against the threat of terrorism.

Therefore, this new model of cooperation among nations is not a utopia, but a vision of the future. The closest thinker in the European philosophical tradition to Confucius, Nicolas of Cusa, created an epochal new philosophical approach, which really separated the Middle Ages from modern times: He said the principle bringing about order and wholeness, the idea of concordance, of a universal concordance in the universe, is that harmony is not an aesthetic thing, but that in a contrapuntal way, the different microcosms must develop each other to the fullest, to the benefit of the other—the "win-win" idea; also the principle of the Peace of Westphalia.

Why is it that some people can see and believe in this vision, and others cannot? It's an epistemological

FIGURE 3
The World Land-Bridge Network—Key Links and Corridors

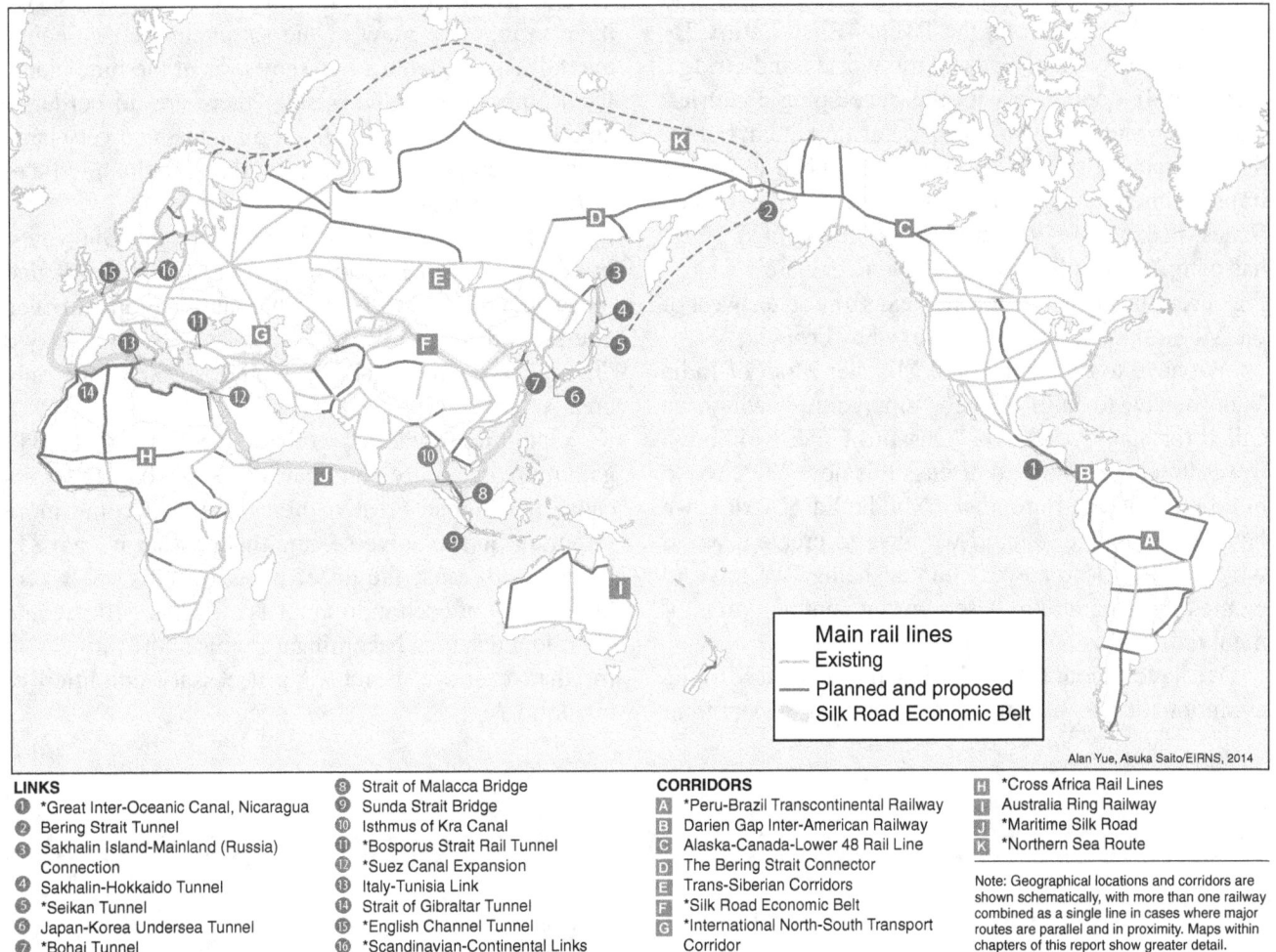

Alan Yue, Asuka Saito/EIRNS, 2014

Main rail lines
--- Existing
— Planned and proposed
Silk Road Economic Belt

LINKS
1. *Great Inter-Oceanic Canal, Nicaragua
2. Bering Strait Tunnel
3. Sakhalin Island-Mainland (Russia) Connection
4. Sakhalin-Hokkaido Tunnel
5. *Seikan Tunnel
6. Japan-Korea Undersea Tunnel
7. *Bohai Tunnel
8. Strait of Malacca Bridge
9. Sunda Strait Bridge
10. Isthmus of Kra Canal
11. *Bosporus Strait Rail Tunnel
12. *Suez Canal Expansion
13. Italy-Tunisia Link
14. Strait of Gibraltar Tunnel
15. *English Channel Tunnel
16. *Scandinavian-Continental Links

CORRIDORS
A. *Peru-Brazil Transcontinental Railway
B. Darien Gap Inter-American Railway
C. Alaska-Canada-Lower 48 Rail Line
D. The Bering Strait Connector
E. Trans-Siberian Corridors
F. *Silk Road Economic Belt
G. *International North-South Transport Corridor
H. *Cross Africa Rail Lines
I. Australia Ring Railway
J. *Maritime Silk Road
K. *Northern Sea Route

Note: Geographical locations and corridors are shown schematically, with more than one railway combined as a single line in cases where major routes are parallel and in proximity. Maps within chapters of this report show greater detail.

---

problem. Cusa makes the distinction between *ratio*, what Lyndon LaRouche calls "practical people," and the intellect and reason. On the level of the *ratio*, the understanding, you have the level of Aristotelian contradictions of what we perceive with the senses. The intellect, however, reason, transcends the *ratio*; the intellect is situated as an indestructible prescience; it is our eye for the search for truth. If we didn't have that, we would not even start the search, or even if we found something, we wouldn't know if that were what we sought. The intellect is an intuitive insight, which allows us to see the coherences and conceptions of causal relations, of connectivities. It is a new method of thinking, completely different from the discursive way of thinking. The Aristotelian practical man, according to Nicolas of Cusa, is like a horse tied to a

feeding trough, who only eats what is put in the trough.

If you are on the level of the intellect, you have to free yourself from established opinions to be open for new thinking. And one has to break free from the trough. "You can't do anything anyway," that is what most Europeans say when you talk to them about that. But it's not true! Why should Europe go along with a policy like the U.S. nuclear missiles in Europe, which only makes Europe the target of its own extinction? Why should we get drawn into another war based on lies? The lies of those around the Ukraine crisis?

The truth must come out of that. It is not enough to oppose the war, but we have to do, maybe what Charles de Gaulle did in 1966: namely, disassociate from NATO. More important, we have to implement these existing solutions. We have to mobilize like *nothing* in our lifetime before, to get the European nations and the United States to join with the World Land-Bridge, and to create a peace order for the Twenty-First century. By joining the New Silk Road and the World Land-Bridge, we not only cooperate with the developing countries, like Africa and Latin America, to develop them, but we need to rebuild the United States! We need to have a transcontinental fast train system across the United States, because the infrastructure in the United States has completely collapsed. We have to declare a war on the desert, because California, Texas, the states west of the Mississippi, are being destroyed by drought.

We have to do what Prime Minister Modi of India said: we have to build 100 new "smart cities," which we called for many years ago, "Cusanus Cities," although it would take too long to discuss this now. We have to build up southern Europe, the Middle East, Africa; we have to overcome hunger; we have to create a world which is livable for every human being. We have to create a new paradigm based on the common aims of mankind.

We have to consciously initiate the next phase of the evolution of the human species, and agree on joint space exploration. All the BRICS countries are space-travelling nations, and Europe and the United States have to accelerate their efforts to cooperate on that. We have to take the view of the astronauts, cosmonauts, and taikonauts, who, when they look at the blue planet from outer space, always say, "there are no borders," and they realize how small our planet is, in a very large Solar System, and even larger Galaxy, in the middle of *billions* of galaxies.

And if we want to exist in 100 years, in 1,000 years, in 100 million years from now, we should prove that those geophysicists who say that mankind only arrived one second before 12, and will disappear one second after 12, are wrong: That mankind, so far, is the only creative species we know.

Vladimir Vernadsky said that the noösphere will gain more and more dominance over the biosphere because the human creative process will become more important in the universe, and that is what we have to focus on. Because the future of mankind is one where the identity of each individual as a genius will become the rule. Each man becoming a genius in the future: But for that to arrive, beauty is a necessary condition of mankind.

The New Silk Road and the BRICS: A New Paradigm for Civilization

After the following four presentations, journalist Christine Bierre moderated a wide-ranging discussion, which included Mrs. LaRouche.

The Vocation of the BRICS, Seen from Moscow

by Leonid Kadyshev
Minister-Councillor of the Russian Embassy in France

I don't want to reduce my speech exclusively to the relationship between the BRICS and "The New Silk Road" project. First of all, because this project has many dimensions, including, among others, great opportunities for cooperation with the Eurasian Union, of which Russia's membership is also very important. Secondly, it is crucial that there be an understanding that the significance and the creative vocation of the BRICS, as a new kind of grouping, isn't reduced to a mere number of selected projects—its scope is much larger.

EIRNS/Christopher Lewis
Leonid Kadyshev

BRICS in the World System

First of all, I would like to address the role of the BRICS in the international system as seen from Moscow. Today, the BRICS are asserting themselves as an influential participant in the world system of governance. At the same time, the BRICS is a young inter-state association which, from a Russian point of view, reflects the great trends of our time. It additionally possesses a number of innovating qualities.

The emergence of this group was the natural outcome of the dynamic development of the processes of globalization, of the scattering of global world power and of the strengthening of new poles of growth and political influence, in parallel with the strengthening of the interdependency of the countries located on different continents.

The cooperation among the "Five" reflects the shared need for establishing a solid partnership between the different cultures and civilizations as the basis for the formation of an international polycentric system. The fact that the phenomenon of the BRICS corresponds to this objective vector of world development, makes this formation attractive, dynamic and future-oriented. It is vital that this group is not tied up in the straitjacket of hierarchy nor the rigid discipline typical of politico-military blocks or coalitions. The BRICS are a symbol of the multi-polar world in the making. It is obvious that, for this reason, the attitude of the West towards the BRICS,—I will make an understatement,—is cautious. The West, used to controlling numerous processes of the world economy, cannot accept the fact that there exist free alternatives.

Cooperation within the BRICS, in our opinion, constitutes an example of the way in which multilateral partnership must be built in the Twenty-First Century. Nobody exerts domination inside this group, there is no submission, and we work on the basis of a true equality and mutual respect. This cooperation is not directed against non-member countries,—on the contrary, we share a positive agenda which consists, above all, in creating additional sources of development and in bolstering the well-being of our populations, which is inextricably related to the objectives of the maintenance of viable international stability.

Therefore, all those who try to accuse the BRICS of being conflict-oriented, are wrong. This isn't at all its true nature.

The defense of the principles of democracy and of justice in international relations, is a key aspect in all the activities of the BRICS. It is one of the main centers of policy formulation, offering balanced positions in the interest of solving the most pressing international problems. In this context, it is difficult to overestimate the importance of the voices of solidarity with the BRICS, calling for an in-depth collaborative effort for peaceful conflict resolution as backed by the UN Charter, without double standards, and without any unilateral military intervention or the use of the "big stick" of sanctions. The defense of the indivisible character of security, and the refusal to admit that it is possible to bolster one's own security to the detriment of that of others,—consolidate the potential of the BRICS to develop long-term solutions to regional crises. This role of the BRICS cannot but grow.

The common approach to guaranteeing that the creation of the new multi-polar system be based on reason, truth and the partnership of civilizations, allows the BRICS to serve as a sort of lighthouse in the turbulent sea of world politics. Another proof of the growing authority of the BRICS is the success of the summits in the "outreach" format, with the participation of the countries belonging to the host country's region. The Russian city of Ufa is preparing to host the next gathering of this type, to which our Eurasian partners are invited.

The coming Russian Presidency

As underlined by Russian Head of State Mr. Vladimir Putin, the Russian presidency will place greater emphasis on the most efficient use of the capacities of the BRICS to strengthen security and stability in the world.

Each BRICS summit is a milestone, a step in the development of this young association. During the Fortaleza summit (15-16 July, 2014), documents were signed for the creation of a New Development Bank (NDB) as well as the founding charter of the BRICS. In Ufa, the Russian presidency is aiming for substantial progress in several areas. It hopes to bring the cooperation of the BRICS to a new strategic level. In the economic field, we are counting on the kick-off of the New Development Bank launched on the eve of the summit, and on the creation of the pool of currency reserves—which requires the completion of the ratification process by all the Member States. The Russian side is hopeful that that will happen, since the ratification process is going very well in all the participating countries.

On top of that, we expect the strategy of the BRICS' economic partnership to be adopted at the summit. It will be a progress document for the pursuit of the development of our cooperation in the pivotal domain,—the economy. Immediately after the adoption of this strategy, we plan to start elaborating a roadmap for cooperation in the field of investments. This document has the purpose of fleshing out this cooperation with interesting and well-detailed joint projects. Another major aspect in the economic field: it is planned that new axes of cooperation will be opened: mining, energy, communications and a number of other areas. We count on cooperation to facilitate the conduct of business: this includes tax policy, simplification of formalities, etc. Significant will be the events prior to the Ufa summit. First of all, one should note that on June 8 of this year, the parliamentary forum of the BRICS met for the first time. The parliamentary dimension will enable the reinforcement of the basis of cooperation among members. Another important element of the Russian presidency, which will enrich the spectrum of the summit—is the Youth Summit, which will be held in Kazan in June. This is also a new phenomenon in the development of the BRICS. The summit will enable us to bring the BRICS closer to the young generation of our countries—we know that any organization has perspectives and a future if it is supported by young people. One should also note the cooperation in the field of culture—yet another new dimension. A cooperation agreement between the BRICS countries in the field of culture will be prepared for the summit.

BRICS and World Development

The question of the significance of the BRICS for the world economy must be given special attention. It is essential for our international partners to understand: the BRICS do not intend to go for a confrontation with anybody whatsoever—neither in politics nor in the domain of finance, nor of the economy. I want to underline once again the Russian vision of the BRICS—it is a proposal to the world of a fundamentally new model of cooperation. Of a model based on going beyond the old lines of division constituted by the confrontation of blocks or by the thinking that is behind it, according to the "East-West" or "North-South" axis.

The BRICS are open to cooperation with all States, independent of their geographic origin or political aspirations. At the same time, Russia is opposed to the creation of closed economic systems that keep the countries of the BRICS at a distance. For instance, the United States categorically refused to consider the question of the admission of China to the Pacific Partnership; the same attitude was displayed towards Russia. In those circumstances, Russia believes that the response of the BRICS should be to support the system of international trade founded on the rules of the WTO, by uniting our forces. The WTO is a kind of United Nations of world trade. If it starts breaking down, it will provoke a severe trade competition, and great antagonisms won't be long to arise. Russia is against such a scenario, and therefore pronounces itself firmly for maintaining a unified system of rules, which is the foundation of the WTO.

In respect to economic cooperation within the BRICS, the Member States are realistic: we see what is happening in today's world. Accordingly, there is a joint desire to facilitate the cooperation between our business communities to the maximum, in order to make use of the great opportunities opened by the complementary character of our economies. For example, the new bank of the BRICS, as well as the pool of currency reserves, will, among other things, help Russia as well as all the other countries of the BRICS, to counter the illicit and politicized pressure of the West. When the bank becomes operational, the work on the major infrastructure projects and investments in the format of the BRICS will follow a growth curve and bring tangible positive results.

The market of the BRICS accounts for three billion consumers—this is more than the potential market of the free trade zone of the Pacific and of the trans-Atlantic free trade zone. Otherwise, it is the most dynamic market in the world. The BRICS need to work to lift the obstacles to their joint trade, and do so on a balanced basis.

Inspecting the New Concept of 'One Belt, One Road

by Shi Ze

Senior Research Fellow and Director of International Strategic Studies on Energy of the China Institute of International Studies, a Think-Tank of the Foreign Ministry, Beijing.

A look at a new concept and the remarkable practice of China's development through the "One Belt, One Road" (as prepared for delivery).

First part

When introducing the magnificent concept of the "One Belt One Road," Chinese leaders already drew the attention of the international community.

The majority of the international community reacted very positively. But certain observers saw in this concept of One Belt, One Road the strategic importance of China's economic and social development, and its diplomacy.

EIRNS/Christopher Lewis
Shi Ze

It appeared that China was only proposing this idea of "One Belt, One Road" in the perspective of its own development, and not as an important occasion and potential to bring growth and development to all the regions of the zone, and even worldwide.

Whoever thinks that the project of "One Belt, One Road" is only meant for the development of China, is misinterpreting the deep meaning of its strategic objective.

Many foreign media interpreted this concept as a "Marshall plan" in a Chinese version and a challenge to the international order of the U.S. This is an even more biased interpretation.

So why did China propose this ambitious concept of "One Belt, One Road"?

First of all, I would like to analyze, starting from the standpoint of a balanced development, why China's promotion of the "One Belt, One Road" is able to promote joint development of the countries along the road?

Concerning how to define a balanced development of the countries along the route, three different levels can be distinguished:

First, in light of the level of development of inland China, the project contributes to a balanced development between western and eastern China, because there is now an imbalance in the development of the East and the West.

As for China's topography, everyone knows that the West is high and the East is low, the West is a plateau and the East is a plain.

However, in terms of economic development, it's just the opposite. The East is on top and the West on the bottom. That is to say that in the East, including in the coastal region, economic development is stronger, while in the West, it is weaker. Economic development in the mountains and in the countryside is relatively backward.

You might say that it is the opposite of the topography.

According to the data recently published by the National Statistics Office, the GDP of China is 6,800 US dollars per inhabitant. While the GDP per inhabitant of the Xinjiang autonomous region on the western border is 6,200 U.S. dollars, the GDP in the Delta of the Pearl River has been greater than 10.000 U.S. dollars for several years now and in certain zones, it is close to 20,000 dollars. That is an enormous difference.

The second level concerns the unbalanced development between China and the countries to the east and to the west of its periphery.

In 2014, the volume of our trade with Japan reached 310 billion U.S. dollars; with the ASEAN countries, the volume was 480 billions U.S. dollars; and with South Korea, it reached 290 billion.

If you add up all three, Japan, South Korea and the ASEAN countries, the total trade volume was 1 trillion U.S. dollars. On the other hand, what is the situation of imports and exports with the West?

In 2014, the trade volume between China and the five Central Asian countries was about 40 billion U.S. dollars; with India, about 70 billion U.S. dollars, and trade with Russia was not greater than 100 billion dollars.

The Russian Federation and India are among the biggest countries in the world. Together with Central Asia, the total trade between China and these countries was not even greater than the amount of trade between China and South Korea, which amounted to 240 billion U.S. dollars. That is why we launched the concept of "One Belt, One Road," a strategic vision oriented toward the west of China and toward the great Eurasian region, so that the development of these regions to the west could become as dynamic as in the eastern regions.

We know that the west of China is rich in resources. The region concentrates a wealth of resources. And the neighbors of the western region of China just as the Central Asian countries, Russia and those of western Asia are rich in resources, for example, in oil, natural gas and non ferrous metals. These are the countries in the world with many reserves.

Currently, China's sustainable development is faced with a bottleneck, which is the lack of resources. Oil imports last year were 310 millions tonnes. 310 millions tons is a very large figure. It represents 58% to 59% of the total consumption of our country, nearly 60%. So it is obvious that China is dependent on foreign countries for its energy.

Therefore, China needs to cooperate for energy and resources with the countries along the road, not only to improve and develop their economies but also for the sustainable development needs of China itself.

Cooperation in energy and resources is not only in the interest of the development of the countries along the road, but is also advantageous for the development of China. The purpose is to serve the interests of the two parties.

The third level is to contribute to the development of all of the Eurasian continent. This will allow creation of a new locomotive of world-wide economic growth.

The Eurasian continent is a vast territory. The eastern part is the Asia-Pacific economic center, which has a flourishing economy. Western Europe, adjacent to Eurasia, is a prosperous economic space.

In contrast, the vast central zone is developing slowly, far behind the two extremities of the continent. The image of this situation is that of a barbell. Big at two extremities, with a narrow strip for the part in between. But it is contains many seeds and offers a enormous potential.

In other words, the two extremities of Eurasia experience rapid development and the central regions have lagged behind for a long time now.

If development of "One Belt, One Road" makes headway, it can build an immense new economic zone, in terms of population, total economy and development potential. None of the current two economic zones can be compared to this zone, which can create a structure which favors the development of all of Eurasia, going through the east, the center and the west of the region.

Acceleration of the development of the Eurasian continent will be an important locomotive for growth of the world economy. It will play an important role in balancing development, to stimulate the world economy.

Second part

China proposed this idea in circumstances in which it faces a great challenge, which greatly stimulated its inspiration and its creativity. The starting point is the development of China and, at the same time, the promotion of development and progress in the world as a whole.

What does the "One Belt, One Road" project bring to the world? In my opinion, there are the following points:

First, it will continue to promote the process of globalization. Over the past decades, the impetus of globalization accelerated the rapid integration of politics, the economy and culture.

The rapid development of globalization changed the political structure of the world economy. The role of states and of emerging economies in particular must not be ignored in the world economy.

Nevertheless, the financial crisis which began in the United States raised doubts in many countries. They no longer see in globalization just a plus for their own development, but also a source of many problems.

Some countries have even begun reflecting on the advantages and disadvantages of globalization. Ideas and actions have even been raised against globalization. Problems are perceptible with regard to trade issues, where the developed countries toughened the trade standards for the emerging economies. Some even waved the banner of protectionism during the multilateral trade negotiations of the WTO.

Likewise, a new phenomenon in the world economy is the decoupling and the tendency to differentiate between emerging countries and developed countries. Economic growth in developed countries no longer reaches the level it used to have in the past, when it pulled along the growth of the emerging economies.

In that context, President XI Jinping proposed the "One Belt, One Road" project to promote globalization. He stressed that China, under the impact of globalization, was not seeking self-preservation, but wanted ties to be forged among countries with their history and their culture.

"One Belt, One Road," by bringing together over 60 countries and substantially strengthening the bases of communication as well as economic and trade cooperation among them, will give a powerful thrust to globalization.

Secondly, it concerns the creation of new locomotives for world economic growth. Europe is an example in this respect.

For hundreds of years, Europe was at war. Twice, Europe caused world wars which had a devastating effect on it. After the idea of the European Union, visionary European statesmen proposed a plan for creation of the euro and the Eurozone.

The birth of the euro in 1999 was a major event in the political and economic world.

Launching the euro allowed for stabilizing prices, accelerating the flow of capital and promoting economic development in the Eurozone.

Since the euro was adopted in international trade, companies no longer have to handle ten currencies, but only one, which makes it possible to greatly reduce fluctuations in the cost of transactions and exchange rates. The euro contributed greatly to the development of international trade.

It brought many advantages to the Eurozone countries. And a stable, prosperous Europe is vital for maintaining peace in the world.

At one of the extremities of the "One Belt, One Road" is the Asia-Pacific economic circle, at the other is the developed European economic space and in between, are countries with rich seeds, all of which has a tremendous potential.

If development of "One Belt, One Road" progresses, it can build an immense new economic zone, in terms of population, total economy and development potential. None of the current two economic zones can be compared to this economic zone. It will be an important locomotive of worldwide economic growth.

"One Belt, One Road" will contribute rapid growth to the construction of the world economy, as development is the solution of the problem of poverty. It is only sustainable development which will be the most efficient means to solve, finally, the problem of poverty and improve the living standards of the population.

Thirdly, it will release the positive energy of different civilisations and develop tolerance. All along the route of "One Belt, One Road," given the complexity of the religions of each ethnic group, we have to maintain open-mindedness and tolerance conducive to resolving the above-mentioned problems.

Chinese culture is characterized by great tolerance. The influence of culture is fundamental. The tolerance of Chinese culture has been crucial in the logic of China's action in the international community.

Chinese culture as inspired by Confucius requires "cultivating oneself and then helping others." That means we should first do good for ourselves and then we are capable of interacting with others. The influence of Chinese political philosophy and culture is the principal and fundamental key of China: reflection inward and tolerance outwards.

This philosophy is very different from others in the world, in particular from western philosophy. Cultures on the world scale are different, but there is no difference in determining good from evil. The diversity in cultures only underlines the richness of humanity. The building of "One Belt, One Road" means learning from each other, practicing mutual tolerance and not pursuing a path toward conflict. These are the products and the capabilities which China hopes to contribute to the world.

Fourthly: help strengthen peace and security in the world. The experience of Europe and other countries shows that close cooperation of economic policies brings lasting peace and security.

The interests of the countries along the "One Belt, One Road" are intricate and complex. The terrain of traditional and non traditional security threats is very serious and it is a fundamental consideration for implementation of the "One Belt, One Road" project.

Setting up a sustainable regional security mechanism is indispensable for building "One Belt, One Road." But the most urgent is the development of close economic cooperation among the countries along the Belt.

Economic integration in itself is an important basis for maintaining security.

President Xi Jinping proposed a new security concept during the meeting of the CICA (Conference on Interaction and Confidence-building in Asia), underlining the need for common security, collaborative security, collective security and sustainable security. This concept could become an important consensus in the launching of the "One Belt, One Road."

"One Belt and One Road" cannot be built without a common, collaborative, collective and sustainable security mechanism; it cannot be built without taking consideration to the security concerns of the major powers, and it must provide security along the sea and land corridors of the Belt and Road to protect the production, contributing by this to the future security of the entire world .

Third Part

What are the innovations in the "One Belt, One Road" proposed by China?

First, it differs, in terms of diplomatic philosophy, from the policy introduced at the beginning of the reform and opening, namely the notion of "borrowing external resources"in the service of economic reconstruction, but it also show that the vision of China's strategy is not narrow nationalism, as some media claim, but has become a form of cosmopolitan thinking.

It is a combination of the development and the capabilities achieved with the reform and opening up to the international system for the past 30 years, and transmitting this back into the outside world, shaping thus a cycle of interactive two-directional development.

This shows that China has really begun to construct a kind of system of "justice and benefit" contributing to the common development of all the countries of the world, including neighbor countries, to share the dividends of China's development.

This practice will become a plus in the interest of these countries. Because it means that China, which is continuing to develop, wants to actively build an international perspective on the basis of the rules in force. It is also in this way that China and outside countries will end up in a kind of polymerization reaction, via the "economic zone of the silk road."

Secondly, during the construction of the "One Belt, One Road," China has made the political commitment to continue pursuing openness, equality and sharing. China's main concern is to form a kind of cultural cooperation with the countries located along the region in spite of the large differences in terms of politics, ideologies and economic models.

One could say it is a distillation of the "Shanghai spirit," which encompasses "mutual confidence, mutual advantage, equality, consultation, respect for cultural diversity and the search for joint development."

It is the reflection of the new geopolitical and geo-economic reality of Eurasia in the post-Cold War period. Its objective is to build and concretize lasting peace in the region, to provide a dynamic mechanism for harmonious development and common prosperity.

That means that all parties are called upon to participate in the cooperation among the stakeholders and to maintain partnership relations, and that any overly egoistical behavior, even if it is not aggressive, will affect the enthusiasm of the partners in cooperation.

In this framework, China's orientation with other countries through a process of mutual cooperation in interests and policy, could stimulate the possibilities of cooperation.

Thirdly, when the obligations and responsibility of China in regional affairs are underscored, that does not mean that China would like to try to dominate them, or even monopolize them, and transform it into some kind of geopolitical project.

Chinese President Xi Jinping also underscored, in his last trip to Central Asia last year, that the essential rule is that China "does not seek hegemony in regional affairs, nor does it seek to manage a sphere of influence."

Although this initiative is focused on ideas for building cooperation among certain countries in the region, China also wishes to maintain coordination mechanisms with other regions and on the international level.

China's initiative to enhance the development of the Shanghai Cooperation Organization and the Eurasian Economic Community, in particular the signing by Chinese and Russian leaders in May of this year of the Joint Declaration of the the "Silk Road Economic Belt" and the "Eurasian Economic Union" is proof of the rapprochement underway.

The initiative of "The Silk Road Economic Belt" is certainly not an absolutely reciprocally beneficial exchange mechanism.

Rather it expresses China's wish to provide, on the basis of its capabilities and other factors, more public goods. It wants to share joint development opportunities with the countries located along the region, promoting mutual development, and then to propose a community of interest along the Belt and to preserve and to promote the existence and continued development of that community of interest.

BRICS: A New Paradigm for a Globalised World

by H.E. Ambassador H.H. S. Viswanathan

Distinguished Fellow, Observer Research Foundation.

Evolution

It is well known that Jim O'Neill of Goldman Sachs, in a seminal paper in 2001 identified four countries (Brazil, Russia, India and China-BRIC) as the fastest growing large economies and hence the best investment destinations. But, over the last 14 years,

EIRNS/Christopher Lewis
Ambassador H.H. S. Viswanathan

the list of good investment destinations has come a long way. South Africa was included in 2011 thus bringing in a member of the great African continent. Today, BRICS represents 40% of the global area, 30% of the global population, 25% of the global GDP and 20% of global market capitalisation.

In the beginning, BRICS had three main agendas: Intra BRICS cooperation, reform of the global financial institutions, and addressing issues concerning global order and global governance. The achievements in all the three fronts have been impressive. There is a robust cooperation in areas of common interest like health, inclusive sustainable growth, gender issues, education, urbanisation, food and energy security, innovation and skills. Intra-BRICS trade has grown fifteen times in the period 2001-2011 and is expected to cross $250 billion this year. This is still a very small part of the true potential that exists. The five countries are exchanging information and learning from each other's experiences and practices.

On the question of the reform of the Bretton Woods

Institutions (BWIs), namely the IMF and World Bank, a small beginning was made in the G-20 Seoul Summit in 2010. Further progress has been stalled by the US Congress.

The evolution of BRICS in the last fourteen years is best described as follows: it started as an aspirational group and in time became a consultation group. Slowly, it evolved into a negotiating group and is now trying to become an agenda-setting group.

BRICS is not only a Government-to-Government activity. New ideas of cooperation are generated in the supporting mechanisms like the BRICS Academic Forum, BRICS Think Tank Council, BRICS Business Council and BRICS civil society interactions.

The Glue that Binds BRICS

This is an oft-repeated question, particularly from those who are confused about the concept of BRICS. The confusion arises because of looking at this group in old paradigms. So far, the world has been used to groups based on geography (EU, ASEAN, SAARC, etc), ideology (OECD, COMECON), commodities (OPEC, Coffee club, iron ore exporters club etc), technologies (NSG, MTCR etc), ethnicity (Arab League), and religion (OIC). BRICS does not fall in any of these categories. Yet, there are some things common between the five countries; they all have played the game of globalisation according to the rules set by the developed countries and have made a success of it. They all have common problems of development and new ones due to globalisation, like unequal growth. They all believe in multilateralism and inclusiveness. They have common aspirations and a vision to have greater voice in global affairs, so that they can contribute positively to global peace, stability and development. Spread across five continents, the five countries are looking forward to building a geography-neutral global architecture. In the past 200 years, the biggest economies were the developed countries.

Also for 200 years, modernisation was the same as westernisation. With globalisation and the rise of emerging economies, this has changed. Yes, there are differences of view on some issues among the five BRICS countries. Which plurilateral group does not have such differences? You might recall that during the heydays of the OECD, there was intense competition between the US, Europe and Japan. Yet, they cooperated effectively on certain strategic issues. Why can't

BRICS do the same? This is precisely what they are attempting—to concentrate on the convergences and reduce the divergences.

BRICS and a New Global Order

What are the changes that BRICS would like to see in the global order? They certainly would not like to overthrow the entire system. Why would they destroy a system which has benefitted them to a great extent? But the fact remains that the global order needs reforms and changes. The post World War II order has become outdated with the emergence of new powers who feel that the existing order has certain biases and advantages in favour of the western developed countries hard-wired into the system. The world has changed and hence there is need to modify the order which should be and be seen to be fair and equitable. The reality is that the geo-economic clout of BRICS is not reflected in the geo-political arena.

As Ian Bremmer points out, "the world has entered a phase of geo-political creative destruction." Both the post World War II and the post-Cold War orders have become irrelevant. Dmitri Trenin rightly says that "life expectancy of world orders varies, but like humans, they are mortal." Many orders in history were changed as a result of wars and violent events. This time around, one hopes that it would be a peaceful process because globalisation has created so much inter-dependence that violent changes of orders are unthinkable.

BRICS would like to address some fundamental aspects of global order. These are recognised principles of values, norms, and rules. For these to be universally accepted, the only optimum route is through a healthy process of multilateralism. One hopes that through these processes, we can work towards a true multi-polar or polycentric world order.

Connected with the question of a new global order is the issue of burden-sharing by the emerging powers, which is often demanded by the status quo powers. Here, it is a question of the chicken and the egg. The argument of the status-quo powers is that the emerging powers should step forward and take on more burdens before demanding leadership-sharing. This, in fact, is the contradiction. The emerging powers have no intention in sharing burdens if it is to promote the existing order or the existing agenda. Why would they do that if it is going to perpetuate the current inequities in the system?

Legitimacy vs. Efficiency

Let me take the example of three global institutions which stand out as being totally anachronistic,—the IMF, the World Bank and the UNSC. The first two, generally referred to as the Bretton Woods Institutions, have outdated voting powers, decision-making procedures, and selection processes for the heads of the organisations. The combined vote share of BRICS in the IMF is eleven percent, even though they contribute to 25 percent of the global GDP in nominal terms and 32 percent in PPP terms. The collective share of BRICS in the World Bank is fourteen percent. Joseph Stiglitz brings out the deficiencies of the IMF and the World Bank in eloquent terms in his book "Globalisation and its Discontents."

It is in this context that the bold initiatives of BRICS to create two new institutions, the New Development Bank (NDB) and the Contingency Reserve Arrangement (CRA) attain significance. Here is an example of BRICS stepping forward for burden sharing. The NDB was a direct consequence of the decreasing availability of funds from the World Bank and other Multilateral Development Banks for infrastructure projects in the developing world. Similarly, the CRA is to address the short term liquidity and balance of payments difficulties of developing countries without the intrusive conditionalities of the IMF. Both these have been conceived as additional facilities to complement the World Bank and IMF, and not to supplant them.

Nonetheless, there is an important political message in the creation of NDB and CRA. They are financial institutions and will naturally work on economic principles to be successful; but, the fact remains that this is the first time in 200 years that a global institution has been created without the participation of the developed west. This, by itself, is significant. Many see this as a wakeup call for other out-dated global institutions. Some even argue that had the World Bank and IMF changed with changing circumstances, there may not have been the need for the NDB and CRA.

The other anachronistic global institution is the UNSC. Even if one grants the logic of UNSC soon after World War II, it is totally outdated in today's reality. There is no question that it has to be made more inclusive with a greater role for the emerging powers.

This brings me to the question of legitimacy vs. efficiency. There is a specious argument given by some that for global bodies to be effective they have to be small. This argument goes against the principle of legitimacy which, along with efficiency, makes the two pillars. Efficiency without legitimacy will eventually lead to the unravelling of the organisation, and legitimacy without efficiency will make it ineffective. Ideally, as Langenhove says, "In all the global institutions there must be three balances, namely balance of power, balance of responsibilities and balance of representation." Of all the global institutions existing today, G-20 seems to be the most legitimate in terms of participation. These 20 countries contribute 85 percent of the global GDP.

Options for BRICS?

In addressing global order and global institutions, BRICS has four options: 1) to conform, i.e., go along with those structures which are fairly equitable. 2) Reform, for example the efforts to bring changes in BWI's, 3) Bypass, i.e., to ignore those norms which are loaded heavily against the developing world so long as this does not amount to violation of recognised international laws, and 4) Recreate; NDB and CRA are examples. Hopefully, there will be more in future.

Outsiders' Perceptions

This is not relevant to intra-BRICS cooperation. But when it comes to the question of changing the global order and global governance, this becomes important because BRICS has to engage others in a constructive dialogue. Fortunately, many in the West see BRICS in a positive light. The sceptics, however, can be classified into three groups: the first group has curiosity; their question is "what is this new animal called BRICS?" the second group is suspicious; it is suspicious about the intentions of BRICS and how their initiatives will affect its interests. The third group expresses hostility; its argument is that since BRICS question some of the existing norms, it could be a dangerous grouping. It is the duty of BRICS countries to reach out to all the three groups and articulate their points of view.

For the sceptics, it would be useful to follow what Jacques Barzun once remarked, "To see ourselves as others see us in a rare and valuable gift, without a doubt. But in international relations what is still rarer and far more useful is to see others as they see themselves."

West vs. the Rest

Whenever there is a discussion on the need for reforms on some aspects of global order, the discourse, unfortunately, is reduced to a "West vs. the Rest" argument. This does not have to be so. Enquiry should not be interpreted as confrontation. Many confuse lack of changes in an established order with stability. But orders collapse when active stakeholders feel excluded (Volker Perthes). If we are looking for an inclusive and fair order, everybody has to be part of it. In today's world, the reality is that the West needs the rest. Therefore, it is high time that we get over the "Us vs. Them" syndrome.

Future of BRICS

As of now, it looks bright. But the main *raison d'être* of BRICS's importance will be the economic performances of the five countries. Of late, they have slowed down by a few points. BRICS will have to register excellent growth rates for the world to keep an interest in the group.

BRICS would work in a practical, gradual and incremental manner. The five leaders are all agreed on this point. Hence, while it may not be prudent to write BRICS off, there is also no need to over-hype the group. Either of these can be avoided if one sees BRICS as it is—that is, as a work in progress and not as a finished product. The intra-BRICS cooperation is bound to intensify and also extend to new sectors. As they coordinate their positions on global issues, BRICS would be able to provide a valuable alternative narrative.

Iran Is Ready To Cooperate with The BRICS

by His Excellency Mr. Ali Ahani

Ambassador of the Islamic Republic of Iran in Paris

The peoples of the world, in particular in the developing countries, are disappointed with the world order that has dominated international relations for decades now, and they cannot tolerate the hegemonic strategies of domination of certain great powers. Moreover, the peoples observe that the difficulties and regional and international crises, far from being solved, have become more complex. In such a situation, the emergence of a new order called the BRICS brings a glimmer of hope

EIRNS/Christopher Lewis
Ambassador Ahani's message was delivered by Majid Javanmard, advisor, shown here.

to the peoples in developing countries.

However, the key to the success of the BRICS lies in their ability to understand the roots and reasons of the bankruptcy and impotence of the old world order. Of course, the lack of a sincere and serious will of the great powers to find solutions to the problems of the world is undoubtedly one of the main reasons for the failure. Properly understanding the roots of the problems and crises throughout the world could facilitate the implementation of the appropriate solutions.

Without a doubt, the Islamic Republic of Iran as a major, inescapable player in the Middle East region, has always played a stabilizing role and favored calming the many crises that are rocking this strategic area of the planet.

As Iran has a decisive geostrategic weight and has large quantities of natural resources (first in terms of gas reserves, fourth in terms of oil), and young and educated human resources, it can be a reliable, powerful and truly independent partner for the BRICS and can cooperate efficiently with them.

The combination of the capacities and potential of the BRICS member countries with the main countries of the different regions in the world, which are able to act independently of the political will of the great powers, will be a key element of success. Therefore, we can be optimistic about the ability of the BRICS countries to occupy the place they deserve, to carry out equal, fair, and sincere cooperation with the developing countries in order to solve the problems of the world.

The Islamic Republic of Iran declares it is willing and ready to cooperate with the BRICS countries, to offer its assistance and support to solve the regional and worldwide problems.

My wish is that the conference of today will have a very positive effect in this direction and I wish you much success.

Thank you for your attention.

Eradicating the Geopolitics of War by Pursuing the Common Aims of Mankind

Moderator Elke Fimmen of the Schiller Institute, Germany began the panel reading two greetings to the conference. The first was from Dominique Revault d'Allonnes, daughter of the late collaborator with Lyndon LaRouche on the Strategic Defense Initiative, Gen. Jean-Gabriel Revault d'Allonnes of the French Armed Forces. She wrote:

I dare to write in the memory of my father. When he met Lyndon LaRouche, he saw the same visions as he himself had, when he landed [in World War II] in North Africa.

The second message was from Dr. Chandra Muzaffar, President of the International Movement for a Just World (JUST), Malaysia. He wrote:

Let me commend the Schiller Institute for organizing an international conference on current developments which will have a momentous impact upon the present and the future.

It is obvious to some of us that as U.S. global power declines, it is becoming more aggressive in its pursuit of global hegemony. The stance that President Barack Obama has adopted on Ukraine is a manifestation of that aggressiveness. While Chancellor Merkel of Germany and President Hollande of France and even U.S. Secretary of State John Kerry seem to show some appreciation of Russia's legitimate desire to protect its sovereignty, Obama continues to insist that Crimea is integral to Ukraine and that Russia is the real culprit in the conflict in Eastern Ukraine. He is in fact endorsing the hardline approach of some of the elites in Kiev which is aimed at igniting a war between Kiev and Moscow.

Similarly, through their angry denunciation of China's reclamation work in a small part of the disputed South China Sea, Obama officials are encouraging certain ASEAN leaders, notably from the Philippines, to resort to even more bellicose rhetoric against China. As a result, tensions are mounting in the region, creating fears of some armed conflagration in the near future. However, Chinese and most ASEAN governments have chosen not to react to these provocations.

Confronted by these challenges emanating from a military superpower that is no longer able to dictate to the world, leaders in Russia and China, and indeed, in other parts of the planet will have to continue to exercise utmost restraint, knowing full well that if they are drawn into the cesspool of war, violence and chaos, they will not be able to offer their people the development and progress that they yearn for. And it is development and progress that China and its partners are promising the whole of the human family through their massive infrastructure projects spanning much of the world.

It is this transformational agenda that will change the lives of millions of human beings. This is where hope lies. The Conference in Paris, I am sure, will re-affirm humanity's commitment to that agenda of hope.

The panelists addressed the effects of the new BRICS financial institutions in moving international economic policy in a new direction. One, Col. Alain Corvez, former French Defense and Interior Ministry consultant, noted: "This conference in Paris is very important, because other countries have not given much attention to the revolution taking place in the BRICS.

"I think this conference will force change."

A Radical Change in Int'l Monetary System?

by Jean-Francois Di Meglio
ASIA Centre, Paris

Conclusion: Between shadow play and domestic debate China is undoubtedly not very transparent and wishes to remain so especially on such sensitive matters as monetary issues. However, it is probable at this stage that two options are maintained by China: Either integrate progressively the post-Bretton Woods system, with the

EIRNS/Christopher Lewis
Jean-François Di Meglio

risks largely identified for a long time and tested during the 2008 crisis; or, invent a cooperation with the glacis of countries that depend on China, are complaisant or share the same ambitions—a new regional and intraregional system, in any case international, but not global.

That system could come out of the new Asian Instrastructure Investment Bank (AIIB), centered on China. Or, around the gas deals concluded with China, eventual first steps towards a disconnection of raw material exchanges with the dollar market.

In any case, the construction of a renminbi zone is on the march. Has it enough ambition to be important enough to impose one day its rules (close to fixed parity between currencies, indexations on underlying, or pegged to something else than the dollar), or is it merely conceived as a protection against a parallel system, distrusted by China, but whose liberal mechanics it uses (notably for its investments in Europe)? This remains an open question at which the debate could bring elements of response.

That being said, one has to note the infatuation created by the Asian Infrastructure Investment Bank (AIIB) for the infrastructure of Europe. China is interested in the technology transfers through the financing of these projects, in terms of infrastructure and non-recourse credit facilities (i.e. credits paid back by the project as such). For the West, the AIIB can offer leverage to access relatively closed Chinese and Asian markets.

However, nothing excludes the newly created AIIB from operating in the future in Europe, where public capital for infrastructure could be dramatically lacking due to deficits. And if these investments will lead the Chinese non-convertible currency to leave its relative isolation, the international monetary system should rejoice about the fact that a system, so far dominated by the dollar, gets more diversified.

Working Together for The Asian Century

by Jayshree Sengupta
Observer Research Foundation, New Delhi, India

India occupies a strategic position in Asia. It is surrounded by China, Nepal, Pakistan and Bangladesh. To its north is Russia. As is well known, the Twentieth Century was the American Century but the Twenty-First century is going to be the Asian Century. But to achieve it we have to eradicate geopolitical wars and rebuild the weak nations in Asia.

EIRNS/Christopher Lewis
Jayshree Sengupta

India and China were the two richest countries in ancient times and, according to Angus Maddison, the two largest economies by GDP output till the Eighteenth Century. India excelled in various fields and its golden age was the Gupta period in 6th Century AD. The British who colonized India for 200 years sent back to Britain huge amounts of money from India, and it became poor.

During the Bengal Renaissance in the Nineteenth

Century, people like Rabindra Nath Tagore tried to rediscover India's glorious past through literature, painting and music. He established contact with Chinese scholars. Reformist religious movements led by Sri Aurobindo and Vivakanada instilled a feeling of nationalism and pride and the seeds of revolt against the British were sown.

The British left India in 1947 and divided the country into two, and Pakistan was born. Acrimonious relations began between the two from the time of Partition.

India and China developed very cordial relations after Independence under Nehru. But there was a war in 1962 on the boundary question that had been drawn by the British. But since China and India have a long history of peace, harmony, sharing of culture and philosophy, they have rebuilt good relations. Since the Second Century B.C., India and China have had contact, and Buddhism was transported from India to China more than two thousand years ago.

The BRICS

The BRICS brings China and India closer together as it gives them a platform to resolve their problems and take a common stand on various global issues. Recently Indian Prime Minister Narendra Modi went to China and President Xi Jinping gave him the Tang Dynasty welcome in his hometown of Xian. Twenty-four inter-governmental agreements were signed worth $22 billion in investments, involving cooperation in various fields. The need for peace and tranquility on the border was recognized as an important guarantor for development and continued growth of bilateral relations.

A huge ($70 billion) amount of bilateral trade takes place between the two countries, and India has a trade deficit of $38 billion with China, a matter of concern for India.

A breakthrough was reached between the two countries on the cultural front. Modi visited the Wild Goose Pagoda which was built to commemorate Xuan Zang, an ancient Chinese monk who went to India for Buddhist scriptures. In Beijing, in the Temple of Heaven there was a Yoga-Taichi event. Three Indian monks taught and promoted Buddhism there 1400 years ago. A program on Gandhian studies was introduced in Fudan University.

China can help India in building infrastructure and in skill development. MOUs were signed in diverse fields like railways, skill and vocational training, mining, establishment of an India-China think-tank forum, climate change and ocean science. The two governments established sister towns and states in both countries.

India can help China in many ways especially in IT, software and pharmaceuticals. Modi said in China, "The prospects of the Twenty-First Century becoming the Asian century will depend in large measure on what India and China achieve individually and what they can do together.

India and China together can help in the reconstruction of one of the poorest countries in the region, Nepal.

Nepal-India-China Cooperation

India and Nepal have been closely bonded since 1950 and today there is virtually no border between the two countries. India and Nepal are members of the SAARC (South Asian Agreement for Regional Cooperation) where China is an observer. Today Nepal is faced with extreme poverty and underdevelopment.

Nepali people are still mostly engaged in low-productivity agriculture which generates low incomes. It has a small manufacturing sector, but it has a fast growing service sector. Nepal scores higher than India in the World Bank's "ease of doing business" index.

Nepal, a country squeezed between two giants, has to be friendly with both. There is a big shortage of power, infrastructure and job opportunities. Nepal's migrant population sends home remittances which form a big part of the GDP.

Nepal has unparalleled natural beauty, a big potential for tourism and mighty rivers for generating hydropower. It is a repository of rare and diverse biological species. It is mainly a mountainous region and has a shortage of arable land. But there are areas where three crops can be grown. On the whole it cannot be a big exporter of agricultural produce, but natural honey, rice, vegetables, herbs and fruits grow in abundance.

Nepal's northern neighbor, China, is facing problems of rapid growth and high rate of urbanization. After three decades of double-digit growth, it is facing economic slowdown, an ageing population and problems of food safety. Its manufacturing growth has slowed down due to slack global demand and high labour costs.

The Chinese government is also deliberately turning away from export-led growth and concentrating on increasing domestic consumption and raising peoples incomes. China is facing excess capacity in its industrial units and infrastructure, but is also looking for outsourcing some of its production to remain competitive. Nepal can fill that role and become a base for assembling machine parts and components, which is becoming more expensive in China.

China is aiming at a more equitable distribution of income and balanced growth between towns and villages.... There can be investment by China in Nepal's agricultural production for it to become a major supplier to Chinese markets. China can encourage migrant labor from Nepal to work in its agricultural sector, as Chinese villages are facing a problem of shortage of agricultural labor. China will be faced with a severe food problem in the future if people keep moving away from agriculture to manufacturing. It has 20% of the world's population but only 7% of world's arable land.

Nepal's physical closeness to Tibet is a plus point. Transportation of food via Nepal to Tibet is easier for China and it can set up food processing and packaging industries on the border between Nepal and Tibet. China's help in infrastructure development in Nepal's northern region can help boost Nepal's own exports to China.

Nepal can also attract more FDI from China which can help in its development and growth.

Nepal's southern neighbor, India, is its biggest partner in trade and investment. India's manufacturing growth has recently picked up after a period of stagnation, and the Index of Industrial production (IIP) was at 8.4% in the last quarter (January-March 2015). Its service sector growth is at 10.1%. India's trade surplus ($2 billion) with Nepal is of great concern to the Nepali government.

India's trade deficit with China can be reduced if there is a good road to China via Nepal. Proper infrastructure will lower transport costs between all three countries. India can outsource some of its production to Nepal which has lower labor costs. There is no language or financial transfer problem between the two and many Indian industries have invested in Nepal. India can set up SEZs [special enterprise zones—ed.] along the Nepal-India border that would benefit both the countries.

In hydropower and tourism, the possibilities for joint ventures and cooperation are immense. Thus, Nepal can leverage the rapid growth on both Indian and Chinese sides, due to its strategic geopolitical location, and ask for infrastructural assistance. There can be joint enterprises on both borders.

For future collaboration between India, China and Nepal, the investment climate in all three countries, especially Nepal and India, has to change. Both need more investment friendly policies with long-term vision and strategy. Nepal needs political stability, strengthening of legal institutions and bridging other policy-related gaps. Nepal can become a New Transit Point economy between India and China. To be able to do so, already 19 sectors with potential for good export performance have been identified. India has to give easier access to Nepali goods and help build its physical and social infrastructure which will help in poverty reduction.

The trilateral cooperation between India and Nepal and China can enhance the living standards of the region. With a total population of around 2.8 billion people, the trilateral cooperation can lead to the emergence of a huge trade and investment bloc in the world.

Pakistan and India

Pakistan is India's most problematic neighbor. Both India and Pakistan have large numbers of people living below poverty. Yet the two countries have gone to war three times. Pakistan is also a member of the SAARC, yet trade between India and Pakistan is small at $2.3 billion, and fraught with many problems, with the gains from trade being denied to the people on both sides. There is still hope that with Prime Minister Nawaz Sharif, trade and investment relations between India and Pakistan will improve. Prime Minister Modi invited Nawaz Sharif to his inaugural ceremony in May 2014. India has agreed to give free access to 300 of Pakistan's export items, and has made the visa process easier and eased the norms of opening banks in India.

While their normal trade has suffered, informal trade has flourished. The informal trade is more than $1 billion, and it has a smuggling component as well as a third-party component, in which trade from India travels via Dubai or Singapore to Pakistan. Smuggling means a loss to the exchequer for both countries, and for third-country trade, the consumers suffer because transportation costs lead to higher prices. Both countries have low human development indicators, rising terrorist activities, and low *per capita* incomes....

The Fight of the Greeks is Universal

by Stélios Kouloglou
Member of the European Parliament for Syriza

Since its election in January, the Greek government has had to face a *coup d'état* taking place in silence. Its intent is to overthrow the new government; to replace it with a government that is docile to the creditors; and at the same time to discourage the voters who are "dreamers" in Spain and other countries, who still believe in the possi-

EIRNS/Christopher Lewis
Stélios Kouloglou

bility of governments opposed to the German dogma of austerity. One kills a government, one kills hope.

The situation reminds one of Chile in the early seventies when U.S. president Richard Nixon decided to overthrow Salvador Allende to prevent that the Chile situation would contaminate other locations of the American backyard. "Make the economy scream," was one of the orders given by the U.S. President to the CIA and other intelligence services before the tanks of general Augusto Pinochet entered into action.

In 1970, the U.S. Banks had suspended all credits to Chilean banks. Today, one week after the January 2015 elections, M. [Mario] Draghi, the President of the European Central Bank (ECB) has cut off, without the smallest justification, the main source of financing of Greek banks, and had it replaced with the Emergency Liquidity Assistance (ELA), a facility far more expensive and needing to be renewed on a weekly basis. Like a sword of Damocles, suspended above the heads of the Greek leaders.

The Debt Swindle

And after the sword of Damocles, there also exists the drug.

Over 90% of the money shipped to us by our creditors returns directly to them—sometimes even as soon as the next day!—since [pledged] to the reimbursement of the debt.

But, in view of the fact that the non-reimbursement of a debt is tantamount to a credit event; i.e., some sort of bankruptcy, the unblocking of the doses is a very powerful weapon in the hands of the creditors, an instrument of permanent political blackmail.

During this undeclared war, other economic weapons are also deployed, such as rating agencies. It is a modern *coup d'état*. As one says in English: "Not with the tanks, but with the banks."

The media have also been instrumental in attacking the government, to evoke the ghost of a GREXIT (Greece leaving the euro zone) in order to provoke panic. Leading this offensive stands, notably, the German tabloid *Bild Zeitung*, which, in 2010, had already started running sensational headlines exposing the alleged laziness and the corruption of the Greeks, who were called on to sell their islands in order to reduce their national debt. The same *Bild* published a pseudo-reportage on a bank run in Athens, showing banal pictures of retired Greeks lining up in front of a bank to cash in their monthly pensions.

Added to this was the media theory about "rescuing" Greece while in reality, by the loans extended to Greece in 2010, it were rather the French and German banks that were rescued. These loans, with high interest rates in the beginning, were presented to German and international public opinion as a free aid to those who were lazy and corrupted.

Let's find out what really happened. According to the French daily *Libération*, since 2010, France made up to 2 billion Euros of profits from interest alone. Even Austria, which participated very modestly, gained 100 million euros up to now, so says its government.

Hence, German public opinion pleads innocence. Except for some TV comedy shows. This is the medium in which they dare to say the truth.

New International Framework Needed

They accuse us as not willing to adopt reforms? But it is us, which more than anybody else, who want to have reforms. Real reforms, not chaos.

What is demanded from Greece is the application of the neo-liberal recipe. Each one with his obsession: The ideologues of the IMF ask for the deregulation of the labor markets and the right of mass layoffs which they have promised to the Greek oligarchs who own the banks. The EU Commission; i.e., Berlin, calls for the pursuit of privatizations susceptible to represent a good buy for German firms (and this, at the lowest cost). Part of the unending list of scandalous sales of State property, is the sale in 2013 by the Greek state of 28 buildings it continues using. Over the coming 20 years, Athens will have to pay 600 million Euros of rent, nearly three times as much as the money obtained by the sale (which was immediately returned to the creditors!).

The Greek government continues to remain highly popular despite some concessions: the non-suspension of the privatizations decided by the previous government (while promised); the postponement of the increase of the minimum wage, the increase of the VAT.

The big question in the end remains mainly a political question. Do elections make any sense, if a country, while respecting the core of its commitments, has no right to modify its policy?

The Greek ongoing tragedy underlines the need for a new framework of international relations. A framework that respects the democracy, the sovereignty and the national dignity of each country, and at the same time favors relations and economic agreements that don't remind us of colonization. A framework advantageous to all players involved. Recently, the Greek government announced it would solicit the participation of Greece in the new BRICS bank, a demand received positively from the side of Russia. In the loaded climate of threats and ultimatums, this really came as a breath of relief and optimism for Greek public opinion.

In a position of inferiority, Athens, abandoned by the forces which it thought it could rally—such as the French government—cannot call for the solution of the major problem which the country has to overcome: an intolerable debt. The proposal [by Greece—ed.] to organize an international conference, like the one organized in 1953 which relieved Germany of most of its war reparations, opening the gate for the economic miracle, has been drowned in an ocean of threats and ultimatums.

Thinking of the Future

The creditors want to put M. Tsipras against the wall with only two choices: financial strangulation if he continues to stick to his program, or betray his promises and fall for lack of support from his voters.

I can assure you that we will resist. We will not be subjugated.

I don't know what is going to happen, but an excel-

lent recent article of Serge Halimi published by *Le Monde Diplomatique* made us think of the future and the historic dimension of this fight.

Thinking of the future reminds us what the philosopher Simone Weil wrote about the labor strikes of June 1936 in France: "Nobody knows how events will turn.... But no fear annuls the joy of seeing those who, by definition, lower their head, raise it now.... At last, they made it clear to their masters that they existed. Whatever will happen from now on, we will have obtained this: Finally, for the first time, or forever, souvenirs other than silence, constraints and submission will float around these heavy machines."

The fight of the Greeks is universal. It is not any longer sufficient that our wishes accompany them. The solidarity that it merits, has to be expressed by deeds. Time is running out.

Multipolar or Unipolar: We Cannot Go Back

by Denys Pluvinage
The French-Russian Dialogue, Paris

Excerpt: The issue of our time is the world order. It is a recent problem for mankind, as before there were limits in technology. These limits have now been surpassed. The bipolar world that existed before, created an equilibrium, because each side was the alternative to the other. There was a real choice. The disappearance

EIRNS/Christopher Lewis
Denys Pluvinage

of this equilibrium is what Putin means by saying, "The disappearance of the Soviet Union was a catastrophe.... The disappearance of the Soviet Union meant that a referent disappeared."...

We cannot go back. Either the EU and NATO win, and Russia and the BRICS countries, possibly including China, are subjugated; or else the disappearance of the American hegemony is a fact. The stakes are very high.

Great Infrastructure Projects Are the Only Real Alternative

The graphics presented with the following speeches are not available at time of publication, but will be posted with the texts when they appear on the Schiller Institute's <u>New Paradigm website</u>.

The Eurasian Land-Bridge of Leibniz

by Christine Bierre, journalist, Paris

Ladies and Gentlemen,

This session of the conference will deal with the great infrastructure projects which are at the heart of the BRICS strategy, and in that context I will speak about the "Grand Design" of Eurasian development proposed in the Seventeenth Century by the great German philosopher, scientist and political figure, Gottfried Wilhelm Leibniz, which is still a wonderful model for today.

EIRNS/Christopher Lewis
Christine Bierre

Before coming to that, however, some remarks about the question of great infrastructure projects. These are indeed, the very basis for the industrial development of a nation. No progress is possible without modern transportation, energy, and water infrastructure.

But, it would be false to look at those projects in themselves, thus risking the danger of falling into the mistakes of Keynesian economists, for whom what is important is to generate economic activity, in whatever area that may be, even if it's only digging holes in the ground to fill them back up again!

What is important in the BRICS strategy is that that infrastructure, and the pulleys, cranes, and excavators used in its construction, are only the concrete expression of human creative genius, and of human will to master the enormous challenges of nature for the transformation of human society.

Before those objects come into existence, there is the conception of man as a creator, opposite to that of man as a predator which predominates today as a result of the varieties of extreme liberalism that the Western financial centers, the City of London and Wall Street, have spread throughout the world.

The BRICS strategy is also nourished by a more noble vision of human civilization, by the will to build a world where all nations, whatever their size and wealth, will have the right to full development; a Westphalian world where all nations will be sovereign to make alliances with the partners of their choice, and not be forced to submit to this or that ideological bloc, or to become vassals of this or that Empire. M. Kadyshev reaffirmed that principle this morning; the Chinese president M. Xi Jinping negotiates win/win contracts every day with small and large nations alike.

This vision of man has unfortunately disappeared in the trans-Atlantic area, where it has been replaced by that of a predator, and by the return of Empires. The vultures are everywhere: in the financial domain, in governments where they loot public wealth and the weakest among us, in war where they unleash their savagery, as in the Middle East.

France once had the opportunity to have a President Charles de Gaulle, who represented in his time the spirit of the BRICS. But now it has fallen into disgraceful opportunistic alliances, where, for a handful of dollars,

France goes from the decadent American empire, to the most backward oil monarchies, without entirely excluding the BRICS however,—because, you never know, they might win in the end!

For the real France, let us reflect upon that 30th of January 1964, when Charles de Gaulle, president of a France just turned sovereign again, broke ranks with the Anglo-American bloc, announcing the reopening of diplomatic relations with another sovereign nation, China. Because, while he didn't approve of China's regime then, he made the bet, as he said it, that "in the immense evolution of the world, by multiplying the relations between peoples, one can serve the cause of men, that is, of wisdom, of progress and of peace... and thus, all the souls, wherever they might be on earth, could meet sooner at the rendezvous given by France 175 years ago, that of liberty, equality and fraternity." In the aftermath of that decision, France left the integrated NATO command in 1966 and opened relations with the Soviet Union as well.

And it is because I am fully convinced that France can recover its age-old sovereignty and break with a western bloc, which the financial crisis and drive for Empire is pushing to world war against Russia and China—and that other European countries can also find there the inspiration to do the same—that I will present to you the immense Eurasian project proposed by Leibniz in the Seventeenth Century.

It is also because this project sets a very high standard, and that in order to succeed in what we are doing, all those who are struggling today to bring about this new world that the BRICS are creating, must nurture in ourselves this beautiful ideal.

Leibniz's Eurasian Grand Design

It was in order to change a Europe devastated by irrational wars and hostage to the demons of religious fanaticism, that Leibniz, a contemporary and collaborator of Jean-Baptiste Colbert, fought to create the conditions for peace and development throughout the Eurasian continent.

Gottfried Wilhelm Leibniz (1646-1716)

Leibniz conceived a "Land-bridge" from Europe to China in the early Eighteenth Century.

His Grand Design? An alliance between Europe and China, the most developed areas at that time, and to let Russia, which is in between the two, progress through the increase of cultural and economic exchanges between them. The relations among nations are not the same today, but the principles remain.

It is that design that Leibniz presents poetically in the preface of his work "Novissima Sinica" (News from China), by saying that:

a particular disposition of providence has made things such that the highest cultures and ornaments of humanity find themselves concentrated at the two extremities of our continent, Europe and China... Perhaps supreme providence, by having the most advanced nations extend their hands to one another, has sought to elevate everything that is found in between, for a better rule of life.

And Leibniz adds that Tsar Peter the Great is favorable to the project and is supported in the endeavor by the Orthodox patriarch.

Leibniz was extremely lucky that both Tsar Peter the Great and the Chinese Emperor, Kangxi, were opening to Europe and showed "a great zeal to bring to their countries the knowledge of sciences and of European culture."

Having worked for years to build a privileged relation to both those heads of State, Leibniz, in his role of counselor to the Princes, attempted to change the course of history. He met three times with Peter the Great (1711, 1712, 1716), and became his advisor. The Tsar had asked him for help to "bring his people out of barbarism."

Concerning Kangxi, the relation was not direct, but through a group of Jesuit missionaries who had been working in China for a century, and who, thanks to their scientific knowledge, had succeeded in gaining the Emperor's trust, and in particular that of Kangxi, who was in power at that time. Leibniz was in epistolary contact with many of those Jesuits, and even inspired the mission of five Jesuit mathematicians who left for China in 1685 to work with Kangxi.

Bringing Progress to Russia

All the memoires of this impassioned dialogue between Leibniz and Peter the Great and his advisors are fully accessible today thanks to the collected works of Leibniz compiled by Fouchier de Careil.

At the heart of his proposals: "attract all active and capable men of all professions"; instruct his subjects, in particular the young ones; teach them how to "create," by rediscovering the great discoveries of the past; translate into Russian the descriptions of all the arts and sciences; open up schools everywhere and create Science Academies in the main cities, Moscow, St Petersburg, Kiev and Astrakhan.

He called for founding libraries and observatories everywhere, and laboratories to build machines.

A century before the British, Leibniz, who collaborated with the efforts of the Academy of Sciences of Paris to develop heat-powered machines, advised the Russians to create a laboratory where the good chemists and pyro-technicians could study the uses of fire for work in the mines, foundries, glass factories and even for artillery. Like a modern day Prometheus, he said: "Fire must be regarded as the most powerful key to the bodies."

Concerning infrastructure, he advised them to reflect on what could be done for rivers and for national planning. To think about the Volga (which could be united to the Don by canal) and to improve navigation especially on the Dnieper and the Irtysh. Make canals to transport goods, as well as to dry up the swamps, he said.

A 'Trade of Light' with China

Leibniz's work in China is also a beautiful example of cooperation among nations, respectful of their best traditions, from which the sorcerer's apprentices of color revolutions in the West could greatly profit.

In his *Novissima Sinica*, he compares the relative merits of Chinese and European cultures, which he finds almost equal. "The Chinese Empire," he says "does not lose out in comparison to cultivated Europe when it comes to land area, and even surpasses it in terms of population." Europe, says Leibniz, is victorious when it comes to knowledge of forms that separate mind from matter, such as metaphysics and geometry. The Jesuits worked to solve that by teaching geometry, astronomy and mechanics,—see the steam car invented by Father Verbiest, tutor of the young Kangxi,—and by assisting in great engineering projects.

But it was the level of daily wisdom of the Chinese that totally impressed Leibniz:

> If we are equal in terms of techniques, if we are victorious in terms of contemplative sciences, it is certain that we are beaten in terms of practical philosophy (I'm almost embarrassed to acknowledge it); by that I mean the rules of ethics and of politics appropriate to life and to the usage of mortal beings. One does not even know what to say about the beautiful order, superior to the laws of other nations, that rules the Chinese in all things, for the sake of public tranquility and of relations among men

This culture of wisdom and of harmony between daily life, political life and the cosmos, was the heritage of the philosophy of Confucius (551-474 BC), enriched by other philosophical traditions. Let us reflect upon the fact that already in the Eleventh Century, China had discovered linear perspective, and that the great art historian Guo Ruoxu wrote in 1074:

> If the spiritual value of a person is elevated, it follows that the internal resonance is necessarily elevated and that the painting will then be necessarily full of life and movement (shendong). One can say that in the most elevated heights of the spiritual, it can compete with the quintessence.

Against the majority of the religious orders and vicars of the Pope who were bent on trying to Christianize the Chinese by force, and who in the end provoked the failure of Leibniz' project, Leibniz supported the ecumenical dialogue of the Jesuits and following an in-depth study of Confucianism, he concluded that a dialog, of equal to equal, could be established between the natural theology of Confucius,—not with the revealed Christian faith,—but with Christian metaphysics.

The mission of the French Jesuit Mathematicians

Finally, to remind those who govern us, again and again, of the best traditions of our foreign policies, let us come back to the mission of the five Jesuit mathematicians to China in 1688 which contributed to found, more than 300 years ago, France's special partnership with that country.

Those Jesuits were the emissaries of the working group constituted by Jean Baptiste Colbert, at the Academy of Sciences in Paris, around the director of the Observatory of Paris, Jean Dominique Cassini. The aim of the group? Use astronomy to correct geographical maps and solve the great scientific and practical endeavour of that time, the definition of longitudes for navigation in deep sea.

Those investigations required the sending of scientists to different parts of the globe in order to collect a maximum of data. The mission of the five French Jesuits in China, was the follow-up to the trips of Academicians Jean Picard to Uraniborg in Denmark, Jean Rich to Cayenne, Varin to the Gore Island and the Antilles, for the same objectives.

Leibniz and Colbert set up the mission around this issue which interested Leibniz at the highest level. In his correspondence on Russia, he described that scientific project in detail, and sets it up as one of his three priorities, calling for such experiments to be conducted in Russia, especially close to the North Pole. The leadership of the team was entrusted to Father Fontaney, who was already in collaboration with other prominent academicians, such as the Danish scientist Ole Römer and Christian Huyghens, who presided over the Academy.

When they set out for China in 1685, the Jesuits were carrying in their suitcases, the tables for the satellites of Jupiter established by Cassini, and some 30 instruments among the most sophisticated of their time. Among them were two machines from Ole Römer: a mechanical planetarium which could reproduce, for any given hour, all the movements of the planets and the stars; and an eclipsorium which indicated the year, month or part of the month where the solar and lunar eclipses would occur.

As a conclusion: If Leibniz was desperate about the corruption of Europe in his time, to the point of having proposed that a Chinese delegation come to Europe to help change things, what would he say about the present situation? Where compared to a China which has made tremendous progress, and a Russia which has recovered its world power status, Europe today is playing the role of the sick man.

I think, however, that the emergence of the New Silk Road, the BRICS and the Eurasian union, can provoke an upsurge in France and in Europe. On the verge of the abyss, on the verge of a new world war, France must quickly renew its dream of liberty, and use these new developments as leverage to rebuild a Europe of the fatherlands, for the greater progress of sciences, arts and its peoples.

Such a change will depend on our actions after this conference!

The Driving Role of The State in Large Infrastructure Projects, But the Failure of Administrative Economics

by Jean-Pierre Gerard
Economist and former member of the
Economic Council of the Banque de France

Summary: "Since 1970 I have dealt with infrastructure, first for the public administration, and then for industry," he said. His intervention centered around three ideas:

1. The state wastes national resources in its intervention, leading to a scarcity of funding for more productive uses;

2. This must lead to a new approach for infrastructure;

3. We must aim at profitability for infrastructure.

EIRNS/Christopher Lewis

Jean-Pierre Gérard

From the time of his university studies, Gerard said, we were taught the so-called Keynesian multiplier, which says that the nature of the investment is not important. He soon realized that it is not acceptable to promote infrastructure without checking its utility. Keynes' theory was formulated at a moment when there was scarcity of money. Today we are in a different situation: The crisis has been created by an excess of cheap money, and it has been cured with the same policy. In fact, there is a monetary surplus in the non-productive part of the economy. There is a real levy on the productive side. QE [Quanhtitative Easing] has worsened the situation.

In the past in France, macroeconomic approaches have generally failed with some exceptions. They have consisted in:

•Horizontal approach: subsidies to production prices. The clearest example is the EU agricultural policy, which was designed to favor France, and ended up advantaging Germany.

•Sectoral plans: steel, machine tools, etc. They have been a dramatic failure and have brought enterpises to extinction.

•Nationalizations: Starting in 1981, there have been many of them: Pechiney, Thomson, Alcatel; none of them survived. Bank nationalizations have also failed.

•The choice of leadership: Managers know little or nothing about the reality of the companies.

Success was scored in the nuclear sector. It achieved the intended aim of energy independence and, although this was not planned, put pressure on oil prices.

The TGV high-speed rail service was a success at the beginning, but then everybody wanted their own TGV, even in areas with low population density, and in ten years the success became a loss.

The Channel Tunnel should have been financed at least partially by governments, and its profitability should have been calculated over 100 years, which would have avoided bankruptcy.

Today, Gerard concluded, we must allow greater economic freedom. The state and other public entities should not engage in activities with no profitability.

Southwest Asia Between Two Systems

by Hussein Askary
Middle East Director of the Schiller Institute, Stockholm

In November 2012, in a similar Schiller Institute international conference in Germany, Chairwoman Mrs. Helga Zepp-LaRouche, stated that she had called for convening that conference on an emergency basis. She said "the reason is, that the international situation, especially in the Middle East, and the possible dangers coming from that region for the rest of the world, made

EIRNS/Christopher Lewis
Hussein Askary

it necessary to have such an emergency conference."

She warned that "the situation in Southwest Asia, or the Greater Middle East, right now, is a complete and total powder keg," and that "if this present trend of politics is continued, mankind is about to crash at full speed into a brick wall."

Ladies and gentlemen, we have indeed hit a brick wall in large parts of the Middle East.

The net effect of the Blair-Doctrine or "Responsibility to Protect", that gives the right to powerful nations to abolish the sovereignty and independence of nations with military means, as most horrifically implemented in the invasion of Iraq in 2003, the invasion of Libya in 2011 and the continued attack on Syria through a combination of Western-Saudi-Qatari-Turkish backing of so-called Islamic terrorist groups such as al-Qaeda and ISIS. The net effect, ladies and gentlemen, has been that large parts of the Middle East today are sent back into the dark ages that followed the Mongol invasion of the region and the destruction of the centers of civilization such as Baghdad in 1258.

Mrs. LaRouche also noted that the purpose of convening that conference in 2012 was "to propose a complete and dramatic paradigm shift, to end the paradigm of geopolitical confrontation and conflict resolution by war," and to "replace it with a new paradigm. She proposed, and we as a team from the Schiller Institute and *Executive Intelligence Review* designed a plan for economic development through connecting the nations of the region with the new Silk Road, and launching a war on the desertification and drought phenomena rather than launching a war on the people of the region. That proposal exists in brief in the report "The New Silk Road becomes the World Land-bridge" commissioned by Mrs. LaRouche and issued in 2014 by *Executive Intelligence Review*.

So, the game is not over, and the chances for a reversal of this process are actually abundant. With the dynamic created by the BRICS nations for economic de-

FIGURE 1

The Nile Basin Initiative is one of many proposals for development corridors in Africa

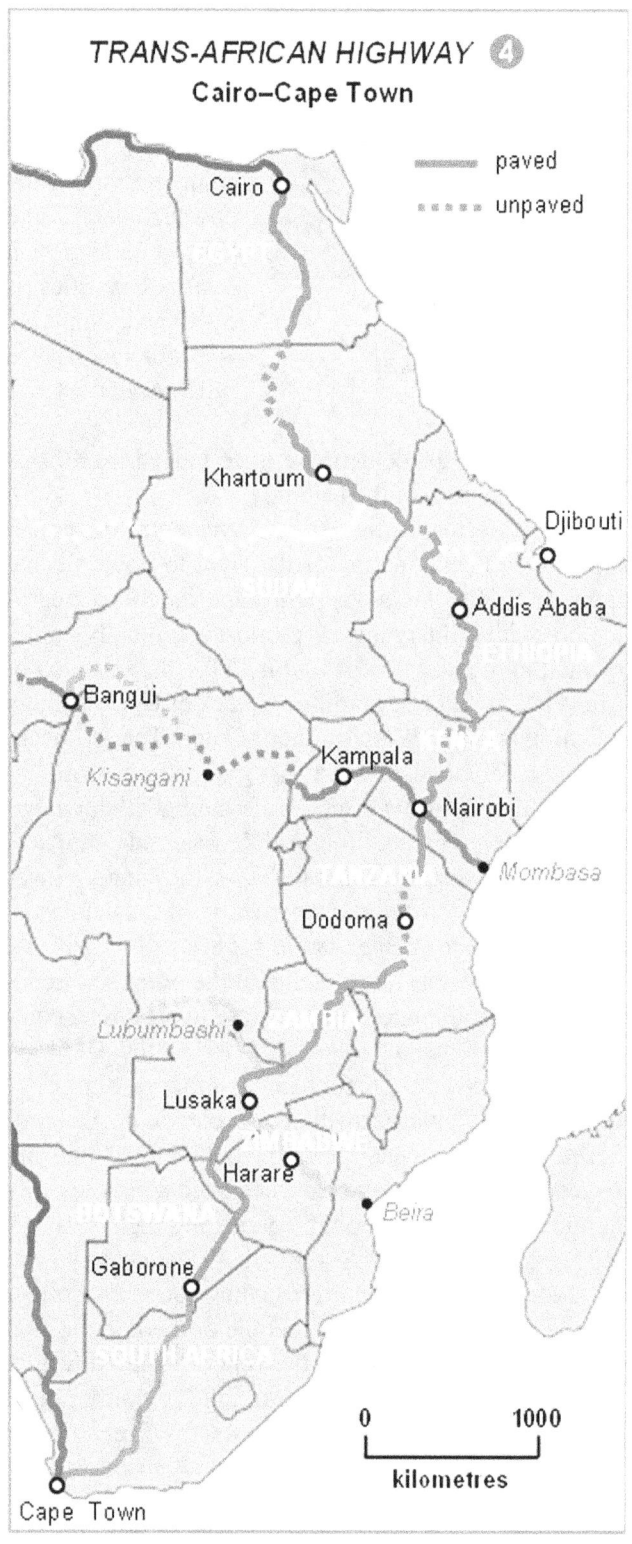

velopment, a new system can be established, based on restoring the independence and sovereignty of nations and bringing them together around economic development and cultural dialog.

Just to inspire you and to bring real optimism into the situation, I would like to give two examples from the region, and one example from the intervention of the BRICS nations, especially China, in Africa.

In the middle of the hell that has been raging in the region in recent years, two nations have been outstanding in their commitment for the development of their economies and lifting their peoples out of poverty. These two nations are Egypt and Iran. Both nations have a great history, great populations of about 88 million people each (most of them are youth and children), massive human and natural resources, and a deep historical and cultural identity. They have been surrounded by dangers of terrorism and war. They have been subjected to economic sanctions and technological apartheid as in the case of Iran, or by sabotage of their economies through policies imposed through the International Monetary Fund, World Bank and free trade agreements with the EU and the U.S. In spite of all that, they kept their head above the water, and their eyes upon the future, working hard to build their economies with the available resources.

First Iran: Iran has made itself an indispensible part of the New Silk Road, as it worked actively since 1996 to build its national infrastructure networks of transport and energy to connect to all of its neighbors. Ports on the Gulf, the Arabian Sea, and the Caspian Sea together with railway networks across the whole country have connected the world to land-locked Central Asian nations, the Indian Subcontinent to Northern Europe through the South-North Corridor from India to Ruassia, and Asia to the Middle East and Europe through Turkey and Iraq. Iran has also persisted in building its nuclear power program in cooperation with Russia.

The first functioning nuclear power plant in the region exists in Bushehr. The Iranian government just announced that it will order a series of small-scale nuclear power plants from Russia to be placed on the coasts of the nation for the purpose of sea water desalination and power generation. Iran has been hit by a new cycle of drought, that historically stretches for 27-30 years. That has affected the massive dam and water infrastructure projects carried out in the country in recent years, which are considered some of the largest per capita in the world today.

The second example is Egypt.

Egypt was subject to destructive economic policies since the early 1980s as mentioned earlier, a fact which made the country dependant on imports of food, fuel, and all kinds of other commodities that were actually earlier produced domestically to a large extent in the 1960s and 70s. Dr. Ali Ibrahim, who will address you tomorrow, is better positioned to discuss this. I have also written extensively on the subject in *EIR*.[1] So, I leave it at this.

The January 2011 revolt in Egypt, which was a reaction to this destruction, was politically derailed and the combination of the Muslim Brotherhood rule and the re-emergence of the so-called Islamic terrorism in the "Arab Spring nations" became a major threat to the very existence of the nation. However, the Egyptian people emerged from this disaster in another revolt in June 2013, and a new leadership and new hope for the nation has emerged.

From reviewing the economic developments and plans for the future that the government of President Abdulfattah El-Sisi have made in the past 9 months alone, it becomes obvious that the thinking in the nation and its leadership is in harmony with the BRICS dynamic and the genuine physical economic interests of the people of Egypt. The building of the new Suez Canal which started late last year with breathtaking speed, is a clear indication of Egypt positioning itself as a key element of the Maritime Silk Road proposed by President Xi Jinping a year earlier. Egypt's relationship to Russia and China especially has strengthened. Simultaneously, its relationship to President Obama's United States and many nations in the EU has diminished.

In the Egypt Economic Development Conference held in Sharm El-Sheikh in March this year, the Egyptian government presented an unprecedented number of infrastructure projects to the world nations and companies to participate in.

Agricultural and industrial development is the key component of this new policy, but it depends on rebuilding the entirety of the nation's infrastructure, turning the country into a hub of transport between three continents. If implemented soundly, these plans will

---

1. See the three-part series on Egyptian development by Hussein Askary and Dean Andromidas in the September 6, September 12, and October 10 editions of *Executive Intelligence Review*. That series references numerous other studies on the North African region.

make Egypt a major economic power in Africa and the Mediterranean Region. Most importantly, they will make a truly independent nation, participating on equal footing with other nations in building the new world economic order. Egypt is also key to stabilizing the whole Middle East and North Africa region. An industrialized Egypt will be able to participate in the economic development of the Horn of Africa and the Great Lakes region, where Egyptian companies are already active.

Regarding the political role of both Egypt and Iran, I personally believe, that unless these two countries normalize relations and work together as the two major poles in the Islamic world, the threat of religious wars will continue to haunt it. As long as Iran and Egypt are seemingly on different sides of the fabricated sectarian Shia-Sunni tension and war, I don't see any clear way of stopping it.

Misconceptions

We have heard and will hear more about the contradiction between the current mindset of the Transatlantic system and that of China and the BRICS nations. The predominant Transatlantic philosophy of geopolitics and zero-sum games, where nations are perceived to be in a perpetual war over limited natural resources, markets and spheres of influence, and the British Malthusian green ideology that is attached to it, has become one of the most terrible obstacles to the development of Africa especially. In dealing with water issues, our team in EIR, have been confronting this matter repeatedly; That alleged population growth, combined with aspirations for economic growth among poor and developing nations lead necessarily to environmental disasters, famine and war. And what do the experts in the Transatlantic propose as a solution? Well, stopping population growth and using so-called sustainable technology, not the technologies used by the industrialized nations.

In 1974 the National Security Study Memorandum (NSSM 200) was commissioned by Henry Kissinger, then National Security Advisor, and was confidential until it was declassified in 1980. It was titled "Implications of Worldwide Population Growth For U.S. Security and Overseas Interests." What it identifies is that: Developing and least developing nations will have a rapid population growth, that will put pressure on their governments to use modern technologies to provide food and other requirements for the their peoples, and that in its turn will lead these developing nations into using the natural resources they have for their own development rather than exporting them to the U.S. and its allies. Hence the threat to the national security of the U.S. and its allies. It proposed to put a limit on population growth as the main solution. It singled out a number of nations for this population reduction policy: Those countries are: India, Bangladesh, Pakistan, Nigeria, Mexico, Indonesia, Brazil, the Philippines, Thailand, Egypt, Turkey, Ethiopia and Columbia.

Let's take Egypt for example: The U.S. spent billions of dollars on birth control programs in Egypt throughout the 1980s and 90s. At the same time, the resources of Egypt were being drained by privatization and the focus on exports. Many people say Egypt is overpopulated.

But Egypt has almost 90 million people living on only 6% of the land of their country, on a strip of land along the Nile River and the Delta. As we have seen earlier, Egypt is getting out of that bottleneck using modern technology, its scientists and its skilled labor.

So, Mr. Kissinger, we have bad news for you. What you feared will happen, is happening indeed. But not in the way you imagined.

We come to the conclusion with this example, as a contrast between the Trans-Atlantic mindset and the BRICS: In May 2014, the Prime Minister of China Li Keqiang visited a number of Western African countries, and later East Africa.

In his tour he offered cooperation with these countries on a large number of infrastructure projects, which these nations are in dire need of.

We have published a series of articles last year in *EIR*[2] on this matter, especially the integration of the water, power, and transport systems of the Nile Valley and East Africa with the help of China and other BRICS nations. It is needless to say that the EU and the U.S. have never contributed to any large scale infrastructure development in these regions. These countries were brutally looted by the British and other empires for more than 100 years. After independence, they had to move from one military coup to the next, and one civil war to the next, but all the while global mining companies and coffee and tea plantations continued to produce and move resources out of these countries. The lack of infrastructure made transport costs in this region

the highest in the entire world. But that is changing right now. The landlocked countries with large natural resources will have the possibility of developing their interior regions, and bringing prosperity and technological development to the population. Their potential will have a chance to be realized.

The map of Africa will change, and is already changing with the implementation of large scale infrastructure projects.

Ethiopia, for example, might never again be associated with famine in news programs, as it has launched a great development program for dam construction, modern irrigation and agriculture systems, in addition to modern transport. It will share the fruit of its massive hydropower projects with its neighbors.

There are great hopes in Africa and even in the Middle East for a different and brighter future, thanks to the positive input of China and the BRICS nations. Europe and the U.S. should participate in this rathern than obstruct it.

How to Rebuild Egypt

by Prof. Dr. Saffie El Den M. Metwally
National Center for Desert Research, Egypt

During the different difficulties that have been facing the region in recent years, due to the great history, great populations, massive human, natural resources, and a deep historical and cultural identity, Egyptians have been outstanding in their commitment for the development of their economies and to combat the poverty. To achieve this target, Egypt firstly

EIRNS/Christopher Lewis
Safieeldin Mohamed Metwally

decided to combat the dangers of terrorism which have been surrounding it from all borders and from their core, create alternative methods to meet their needs from water and energy, and launched many major projects depend on the modern technologies.

At this point, Dr. Metwally illustrated several proj-

2. Hussein Askary, "A Revolutionary Development Plan for the Near and Middle East," in *EIR*, December 7, 2012. also consult www.schillerinstitute.org.

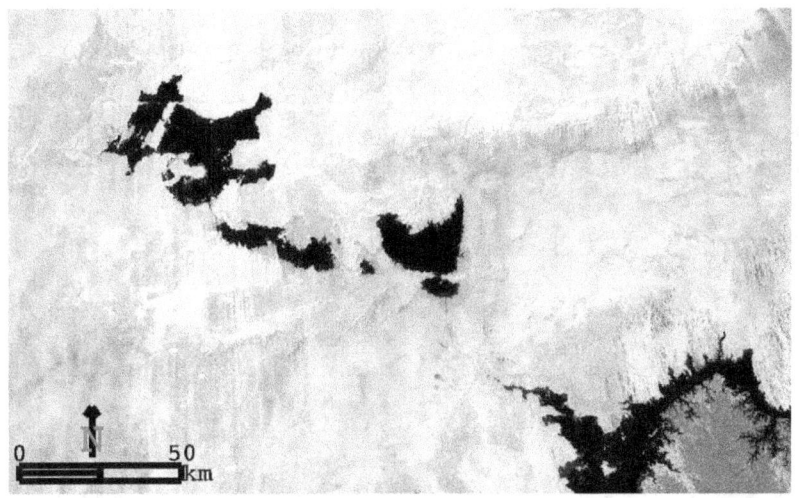

A NASA landsat photo of Toshka Lakes

Creative Commons

Creative Commons/Remih

The new town of Toshka in the New Valley Project (2009). The project was begun in 1997.

ing with other nations in building the new world economic order. Egypt is a key to stabilizing the whole Middle East and North Africa region. An industrialized Egypt will be able to participate in the economic development of the Horn of Africa and the Great Lakes region, where Egyptian companies are already active.

Demand for freshwater and energy supplies in arid and semi-arid countries worldwide is on the rise, because of increasing populations and limited water supplies. This problem is exemplified in the countries of Saharan Africa (North Africa) and the Middle East, where scarcity of water resources is contributing to political instability, disputes, and conflicts. Sources of freshwater in these areas include the surface runoff (e.g., the Nile River in Egypt and Sudan) that generally originates from allochthonous precipitation over distant mountainous areas with wetter climatic conditions. Other sources of freshwater in these arid and semi-arid areas include non-renewable groundwater resources originating as autochthonous precipitation that recharged the aquifers in previous wet climatic periods. For example, the Nubian aquifer that occupies large areas (about 200,000 square km) in northern Sudan, eastern Libya, and Egypt (Hess et al., 1987) is believed to have been recharged during wet climatic conditions in the Quaternary (e.g., Thorweihe, 1982). These fossil waters are currently being used for irrigation purposes in the Dakhla, Kharga, and Farafra Oases in Egypt, and an extensive program is being developed in Libya to extract and utilize these fossil waters from the Kufra, Southeast-Sarra, Tazerbo, and Sarir areas. Because of the non-renewable nature of these waters, the artesian wells fed by this aquifer are drying up, and the depth of the water table in these areas has been steadily increasing.

Egypt is facing increasing water needs, demanded by a rapidly growing population, by increased urban-

ects his center is working on:

•*Land reclamation of half a million hectares in the Western Desert, and the construction of five new agricultural centers and cities. Satellite remote sensing is used to detect underground water reservoirs.*

•*Use of radar technology to detect land mines from World War II over a large area amounting to three small countries.*

•*Fighting desertification in the Sinai Peninsula, thus also helping in eradicating terrorism which has its bases there.*

•*Exploring for minerals and metals in the Eastern Desert.*

They dream to make Egypt a major economic power in Africa and the Mediterranean Region. They try to be a truly independent nation, participating on equal foot-

ization, by higher standards of living and by an agricultural policy which emphasizes expanded production in order to feed the growing population. As described earlier, Egypt primarily depends on the River Nile as its primary renewable water resource. With the adoption of progressive agricultural projects to channel River Nile water to the deserts of Egypt, such as the El Salam and Tushka Canals, Egypt is approaching full utilization of its River Nile water allocation (55 million cubic meters). Thus, there is a real sense of urgency to develop alternative renewable groundwater resources in Egypt in order to cope with the ever increasing fresh water demand.

EIRNS/Christopher Lewis

Acheik Ibn-Oumar

There were reasons for choosing Egyptian deserts as an appropriate location to conduct this project which could possibly be implemented over other arid regions across the world. First, Egypt's landscape and its climatic and hydrologic settings are ideal for the study and resemble those in neighboring countries. Hence, results obtained in Egypt will be applicable to many neighboring countries. Secondly, like many arid countries, Egypt major source of water is surface water in the form of Nile River and Nubian Aquifer as fossil water.

Refilling Lake Chad With Water: A Large Project for BRICS?

by Acheik Ibn-Oumar
Former Foreign Minister of Chad

Acheik Ibn-Oumar presented the idea of Transaqua, the plan developed by the Italian engineering firm Bonifica to refill Lake Chad and at the same time build an integrated infrastructure in Central Africa. Lake Chad is today one-thirteenth the size it was 50 years ago, Ibn-Oumar said. This is dramatic for the conditions of life of 30 million people who live there and depend on fishing, agriculture, and cattle-raising.

Transaqua involves a 2,400 km navigable canal, which would collect water from the eastern tributaries of the Congo River, enough to refill Lake Chad to its original dimensions. The project would create dams and ports, supply electrical power, and promote agricultural development.

Opponents of Transaqua use economic, environmentalist, and governance objections. Some claim that Lake Chad does not shrink, that there is historical evidence of the lake shrinking and returning to its dimensions. This is true, but we are talking about geological cycles of maybe 6,000 years. We cannot wait that long.

Opponents say that it is expensive. But Marcello Vichi, author of Transaqua, calculated that Africa spends $20 billion dollars every year in wars, whereas $2 billion a year would be needed for Transaqua.

Obstacles can be overcome with methods, but in all these years, there has not even been a feasibility study done for Transaqua. Mr. Ibn-Oumar repeated the proposal he made last February, that the BRICS promote the project.

Human Creation, Source and Measure of the Real Economy

by Jacques Cheminade

June 14—Introductory Remarks before Panel IV

God laughs at those who deplore the effects of causes they cherish.

Bossuet's curse of the Seventeenth Century has the merit of striking today at the countries of Western Europe and North America, where people are stirred up with the statistics and apparent forms—the increase of unemployment, lack of social equality, drug consumption, and money and weapons trafficking—without uprooting that which would allow them to bring them to an end.

Oligarchies keep peoples in a state of voluntary submission in effect, and fake the environment in which they operate. To increase the Gross Domestic Product of the EU member states, the European accountants demand that from now on, countries must include in their statistics the revenue generated by all sorts of trafficking. By the magic of the markets, prostitution, for example, is no longer a human tragedy or a burden on society, but becomes a profit appearing on the balance sheets. The precept of Mandeville, according to which the sum of private vices is a public virtue, dominates the entire scope of western behavior, up to the point of making human labor an "adjustment variable," and making profit generated to the detriment the exploitation of human labor, the supreme reference for the markets.

Our trans-Atlantic region is in this way dominated by an incestuous relationship between banks from Wall Street and the City, and the large cartels of cyberindustry, nicknamed the seventh continent of GAFA, meaning Google (G) for cartography and databases, Apple (A) the internet provider, Facebook (F) the social networker, and Amazon (A) the bartender of culture.

That system gambles without producing, and does so at the speed of light. High Frequency Trading (HFT) outside any legal control, operating on alternative platforms of global shadow banking, has reduced the insti-

EIRNS/Julien Lemaître

Jacques Cheminade

tutions of Nation-States to the servitude of debt, and individuals to the enslavement to the desire to possess, by finding out not merely what we do, but by attempting to predict what we will do, and even to know it before we do, thanks to a multitude of data about us accumulated without our consent on the web.

The Pathology of the System

This predatory society makes up a modern version of the British Empire, but with the same destructive impulses as those resulting from the fusion of the British monarchy and the East India Company. It carries within itself war as rain clouds carry the storm, because its predatory character makes it incapable of producing the resources required for future generations. Hence, for one euro or dollar produced, it creates at least four Euros of debt and an accumulation of debt titles without historical precedent.

We know the official figure of financial derivatives, which are gambling claims on future prices which are traded independently of the possession of the underlying asset: 800 trillion dollars, or more than ten times the entire world's annual production. The real figure of all these accumulated money claims, which nobody can determine with certainty since the cross-engagements among financial institutions are managed by computers operating at speeds counted in billionths of seconds, is undoubtedly far in excess of two quadrillion (million billion) dollars!

We have really come to "mad finance" in the primary meaning of the term, but also the madness of a pathological killer. It destroys the human capital on which the entire society is based. Countries such as the United Kingdom, the United States or Germany feign to have fewer unemployed, but have in reality suppressed them by statistical manipulation and organized hardship.

Under these conditions, a climate of war has been born, which the Pope rightly denounced in Sarajevo. We are living in an "Empire that kills," he said already some months ago. The folly of finance is genocidal. More and more officials, from China to the United States, and especially Russia, compare the current situation with the 1962 Cuban missile crisis; the only difference being that this time, it is the United States, the United Kingdom, and NATO which have deployed their forces and nuclear missiles on the borders of Russia, violating everything they promised at the time of German reunification.

Two factors make the situation in which we are now, infinitely more dangerous than in 1962. The first factor is the fact that the majority of citizens do not mobilize any longer against the coming war, or against the looting of their existence. And when they do mobilize, they do it because they have their backs against the wall of their exploitation and exclusion, as in Greece or in Spain. They reject what should be rejected, but have no project to achieve what is necessary.

Yet, if we want to re-establish a world of real growth and mutual development, we have to offer to the impetus of the BRICS countries and their associates, an accrual of power and a larger horizon. We cannot simply say we're going to get on the train of the BRICS and wait till they take us to a good place! That's already better than remaining on the platform, or obstructing them as the oligarchs desire us to do, but it isn't up to the level of the challenge, our challenge and theirs.

We have to contribute the best of ourselves, since it is the economic orientation of the entire world which we have to change. It is not this or that element of the current system which leads us to disaster, but the entire logic of the system itself. We have to change the system. That change is the precondition of a future peace, a capacity to create the conditions of a harmonious mutual development based on the win-win principle, as underlined repeatedly by the Chinese President Xi Jinping.

What a Real Economy Is

Therefore, we really need to understand what economy really is. It is in reality the conception of what a human being really is, which we have to rediscover in ourselves. Human beings are not geopolitical animals trying to occupy territories or control resources to the detriment of other human beings, but instead those who define themselves by their capacity to discover the principles of the universe they inhabit, and to modify the environment through the application of discoveries to allow themselves and their fellow humans to grow and multiply towards a better existence.

That means economy doesn't mean buying cheap and selling dear, and having a financial gain, but the construction of platforms of mutual development to produce more and better with less, thanks to technological applications derived from discoveries. It means increasing our productivity per capita, per surface area and per unit of matter employed in these processes. These platforms incorporate the means to guarantee this dynamic: human infrastructure, education, health and R&D and physical infrastructure, transportation and production units. U.S. political statesman and economist Lyndon LaRouche called this capacity of the human individual, the potential relative population density, relative to the technological and human platform which has been set up.

This notion of potential, of capacity per human being, has been taken up by the Russian friends of LaRouche. The Russian scientist Pobisk Kuznetsov proposed to call it the "La," an economic unit measuring the applied and verified impact of human creation. You now understand why I called my intervention, "Human Creation, Source and Measure of the Real Economy."

It is crucial to underline that with their conception of "one belt, one road," of the terrestrial and maritime New Silk Road, the Chinese experts and leaders are expressing the same conception of the human being. As far as my understanding goes, the concept of the *shi* evaluates the potential to be developed. We no longer require any longer a pre-established detailed plan, but consider situations as a mine to explore, whose veins we're going to exploit with a transformative idea, operating in such a fashion that at the point I engage my action and my combat, I've already won, since I've prepared the conditions to win over my enemy, by transforming him into my partner. Indian Prime Minister Narendra Modi showed that he fully understood this principle when he declared at the conclusion of the BRICS summit in Fortaleza last July:

> The uniqueness of THE BRICS as an international institution [is that] for the first time, it brings together a group of nations on the parameter of future potential, rather than existing prosperity or shared identities. The very idea of BRICS is thus forward-looking. I believe they can offer in this way new perspectives and ways to function for the existing international institutions.

EIRNS
Lyndon LaRouche elaborates his Triple Curve pedagogy in a speech in 1998.

This conception of the economy is radically the opposite of Aristotle's formal logic based on the "principle of non-contradiction," according to which an enemy is an adversary to be destroyed. While for us, an adversary is some one to win to your cause, on condition of elevating the debate. As Nicolas of Cusa underlined the matter, creation supposes the "coincidence of opposites," which makes knowable and controllable at a higher level of conjecture, what on a relatively lower level appeared as unknowable and uncontrollable.

Confucius, with his conception of the *ren*,—i.e. the advantage given to the other, allowing him to acquire the mandate of heaven by instructing him,—develops an approach of a similar nature. Contrary to the current Malthusian nonsense which pretends that "the history of a finite world has begun," Jean Bodin, in his *Six Books on the Republic*, in the footsteps of Cusa, states that, "There is no wealth nor strength but man,"—provided that that a leader makes "accords from discords," an aspiration for unity in diversity whose principle runs as a red line through Chinese civilization.

What We Have To Share

Hence it is clear that we Europeans and Americans have a lot to share with the BRICS, and even to contribute to them. In France, the reign of King Henri IV, with Sully, Laffemas and Olivier de Serres, in Germany, with the Enlightenment of Lessing and Mendelssohn

and the concept of National Economy of Friedrich List, and in the United States, with the Hamiltonian conception of political economy. It is there that there appeared most clearly a sense of economy and of a society driven by a vector of scientific progress and not by the submission to a tradition.

In two of his four founding reports of the "American System of Political Economy," Hamilton shows that public credit, organized by a National Bank, is the foundation of an economy, since it represents a "bet on the future," on the capacity of future investments to produce the means to reimburse the debt incurred. The future of the United States, he understood, was in manufacturing, i.e. industry supported by public credit, and not in agriculture as wanted by Jefferson, since it is industry which can increase the quality and the quantity of human labor. It is the increase of the density of the flows of energy and technology which permits this "physical surplus," allowing reinvestment in still a higher level of future human creation.

In his "Report on a National Bank," Hamilton demonstrated in particular, to the great astonishment of the other founding fathers, how debt can be transformed into money, allowing the emission of public credit. The National Bank was conceived of as a receptacle for deposits coming from various income of all origins, including from titles of the federal debt, which could be capitalized and lent to investors.

In that way, the debt served as a guarantee to circulate money credit and avoid the control over the American economy by foreign interests, emphatically British. Needless to say, these deposits could not be seized and the debts could not transformed into shares of the bank as many would like to do today in Europe, in order to bail out speculative bankers. This was all about the real economy, dealing with projects that produced productivity, and not financial gambling to expand private banks to the point they become systemic, which means that their size allows them blackmail the government to prevent their bankruptcy, and to demand help from the state in case of difficulties, to the detriment of peoples.

This reference is essential today in dealing with the issue of the current Greek public debt. In respect to the criteria defined by Hamilton, and in respect to the debt cancellations granted to the German Federal Republic in 1953, we have to add the separation of reimbursable and legitimate debts from those debts that are not. Scarcely ten percent of the debt incurred by Greece was in the interest of the people and the economy; the rest only benefitted the internal compradors, and even more so, the external financial speculators, who unduly demand their "pound of flesh" today. If there is negotiation, it should involve this point, and not the tourniquet imposed on the Greek population and the economy by the "institutions," in the form of an austerity that amounts to bleeding a body that was already made sick.

In short, what is needed is: A platform for taking off and development, great infrastructure projects, public credit, energy and technology flux density, inspiration and support. Charles de Gaulle, in a speech given in Lille on Oct. 1, 1944, said, when speaking about ending the war:

We want to pool everything we possess on this Earth, and to succeed in doing so, there is no other way than what we call the directed economy. We want the state to lead the economic effort of the entire nation for the benefit of all, and to ensure that the life of every French man and woman becomes better.

Earlier, in Algiers on May 1, 1944, he said:

Great human affairs can not only be settled by logic. One needs the atmosphere that can only be created by the agreement of sentiments.

You also need a lot of courage, which, fortunately, is contagious. This is what Franklin Delano Roosevelt had to say in New York's Madison Square Garden on Oct. 31, 1936, about his enemies, who were the same as ours are today: "They are unanimous in their hate for me—and I welcome their hatred."

A direction, an inspiration, and a sentiment: that was the "detente, entente and cooperation" among peoples of General de Gaulle. This is what Valentina Matviyenko, President of the Russian Federation Council, calls today "a certain format of cooperation between the five BRICS countries that have a common agenda," including:

defense of their national sovereignty, the protection and promotion of their national interests on the basis of the principles of equality, non-interference into their respective internal affairs, and the refusal of a unipolar world.

That is what is prompting China to agree with India and Russia, to open access to its Asian Infrastructure Investment Bank (AIIB) for investments in infrastructure in Japan and in the United States, in spite of historical litigation and unfriendly actions of both of them. That is also what has prompted Chinese interests to open a trans-oceanic canal in Nicaragua, to invest 50 billion dollars in Brazil, and to finance a railroad, again a trans-oceanic one, between Brazil and Peru. And this is what has inspired the Russian Central Bank to propose a new bank clearing system similar to the Western Swift system.

Are We Capable of Change?

Let us consider for a moment the economic changes for the past 100 years. China was the only country which did not sign the Versailles Treaty in 1919, because it had been stripped of its territory. China was not even invited to the San Francisco Conference after World War II, although it had fought with great courage against Japan. Once we are aware of what China has had to suffer worldwide, we can better understand the sympathy it has for Greece today, and for Russia.

Because what we are inflicting upon Greece today, we of the European Union, is what we inflicted yesterday on China. Are we capable of changing? Are we capable of understanding that what is happening to Greece today, can happen to each of us if we do not change policy? Voices are being heard in Germany, as we heard, to ask for Russia to be invited back to the G8. That is more in our interest than in Russia's interest, because the latter is linked to the BRICS, that is to say, to more than half of mankind. Are we able, as Europeans, to avoid a new war? The test will be what we can do for Greece, and de facto for ourselves.

Economics means to recreate the conditions of a will to live together, by bringing together our creative competences and making the whole greater than the sum of its parts. Today, in the skies of Eastern Europe and above the South China Sea, if two planes come too close to each other, everything can degenerate. Today, the depopulation policies have started. And faced with the waves of migration, the only idea which our countries can come up with, is bombing the ships transporting the refugees, and starting a new colonial expedition. Are we so stupid as to accept going down into a barbarism which is deadly for the others and suicidal for ourselves? Economics means recovering the creative goodness of Aeschylus' Prometheus, offering to all the possibility of growing and multiplying thanks to a greater mastery of science, beyond everything known, and finding new vigor by reminding ourselves of our best accomplishments.

Economics means doing for peace through mutual development in the Twenty-First Century what we did for war in the Twentieth Century, i.e. radically changing, overnight and from top to bottom, our way of thinking and conceiving the world.

A new economy will be the smart cities of the future, digital technology freed from financial domination, and not a fatal destruction of jobs as anticipated by the experts, but the foundation of a new economy associated with new, higher forms of energy density, such as controlled thermonuclear fusion power. No solution can lead us back to the past. It is only by re-establishing confidence in their own creative powers, and rejecting their exploitation by their oligarchic masters of the trans-Atlantic zone, that our fellow human beings will rise to the level of the challenge of our epoch. Space exploration and colonization will necessarily play a fundamental role as a common objective for mankind, to escape from our earthly cradle.

However, all of this will not happen through mere fate or mechanically. The reality is subjective. We have to recover the courage of Victor Hugo, who, in 1861,

Victor Hugo (1802-1885) as photographed by Étienne Carjat.

denounced the sacking of the Summer Palace in Beijing, the garden of vortexes of clear water and the gardens of perfect clarity, constructed by the Qianlonq Emperor and the Jesuits:

> One day two bandits entered the Summer Palace. One plundered, the other burned. Before history, one of the two bandits will be called France; the other will be called England. Mixed up in all this is the name of Elgin, which inevitably calls to mind the Parthenon. What was done to the Parthenon was done to the Summer Palace, more thoroughly and better, so that nothing of it should be left.

For having done that, we owe to China that we enter with her into the future, not to destroy but to rebuild the world in the BRICS era. Let me nevertheless tell you that I'm proud of the fact that Hugo's letter is on the official Chinese websites and on the internet, translated into Mandarin. Now I myself want to speak about what we are doing to Greece and the refugees coming from Africa, with the same anger, as inspired by that of Victor Hugo.

However, there remain reasons to be optimistic and

reasons to hope. First, because it is the BRICS which from now on will define the tuning of the world orchestra, and a new drive towards political change is manifest in Europe, including in those countries where the physical economy remains relatively robust, such as in Germany as we have seen yesterday, and also in the United States with our own political movement and the candidacy of the [Martin] O'Malley, who took a stand against the bandits of Wall Street, and is calling for a new Roosevelt-style Glass-Steagall.

Looking into this room, I see we have friends and fighters for this idea from the entire world. So we can hope that the Silk Road will arrive among us, and that we can make it a common objective for mankind in its way of conceiving the world by walking the unknown path, both in our own heart, as well as in the growing mastery of what is taking place inside the solar system and our galaxy, because it is there,—yes clearly there,— as the next speakers will demonstrate, that lies the economy, the real one,—that of our future.

Since I evoked Victor Hugo, let's ask him for more. Confucius teaches us one has to tease and challenge our friends to oblige them to rise above the contradictions of a given situation. It was also in June, 130 years ago,

that he entered our Pantheon. Let's listen to what he wrote in *Lux*:

> O vision of the coming time!
> When man has 'scaped the trackless slime
> . . . .
> Upon the sky-line glows i' the dark
> The Sun that now is but a spark;
> But soon will be unfurled—
> The glorious banner of us all,
> The flag that rises ne'er to fall,
> Universal Republic of the World!

Simone Weil, our great Platonic philosopher, once said that in all labor resides a part of poetry, since real human labor is always creative. Here's the labor before us.

To someone who asked me why Helga Zepp-La-Rouche and the Chinese leader had both hit upon what he thought was the strange name, "the New Silk Road," I answered: it was only natural for them, since the economy is based on creative human labor, and work is pregnant with poetry. And that is what we tell the world which gives its verdict.

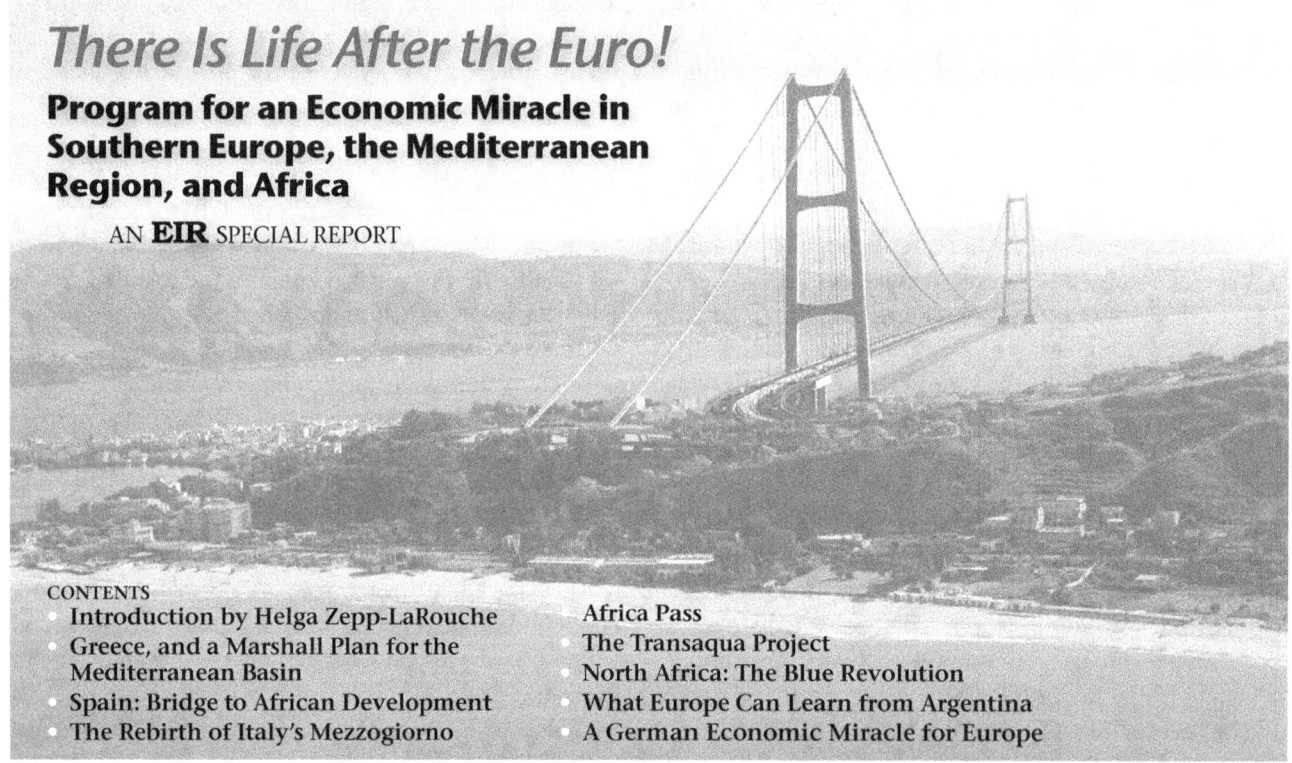

Public Credit and Debt Cancellation, The Political Challenge for Europe

Moderator Karel Vereycken, Schiller Institute, Paris: "The speakers are aware that European nations must join the BRICS dynamic, bringing with them the best of their respective cultures and historical achievements to expand its scope. The crucial issue is to put an end to monetarism and establish a public credit system, both nationally and internationally, to finance great infrastructure projects."

Greetings to the Panel

The panel received greetings to the Paris Conference from:

EIR Founding Editor and economist Lyndon LaRouche *(Transcript P. X)*

U.S. Representative Walter Jones of North Carolina *(Transcript, P. X)*

State Senator Richard Black of Virginia *(Transcript, P. X)*

Precedent: The 1953 London Debt Conference

by Karel Vereycken
Schiller Institute, Paris

Summary: Greece is facing a June 30 cutoff date for payments to the Troika. You must cut your pensions, they are told, and create a budget surplus. They want to kill people to save the equations of the rating agencies and the IMF.

Greece says this is unacceptable, and they have not compromised as of yet. In order to pay the debt, Greece must become a productive nation.

Now the default of Greece is on the agenda, but it is the financial system which has been in default. Prime Minister Tsipras has been calling for debt cancellation and reorganization—to negotiate a combination of a moratorium, rescheduling, cancelling parts of the debt, and to reduce the interest rates.

EIRNS/Christopher Lewis
Karel Vereycken

What are the precedents?

There have been 169 debt cancellations and moratoriums since 1946. Argentina had the largest "haircut," of 65% of the private debt. Iraq cut the Saddam Hussein-era debt, but destroyed the country. In Ecuador in 2006, an audit showed that 85% of the debt was illegitimate. The state bought the debt and threw it out. There was Iceland in 2008, where the banks were ten times bigger than GDP. Icelanders refused to assume the debt.

In 1953, a London Debt Conference was held about dealing with Germany's debt remaining from the Versailles Treaty after World War I, and incurred during the 1930s and through World War II. The London Debt Conference was organized by Hermann Abs of Deutsche Bank. 50% of the total debt was scrapped.

One of the principles adopted was that debt payments should never amount to more than 5% of Germany's exports. The world had to help build up productive capacity—not punishment.

This agreement treated both the private and public debt. (In Greece today: 10% of the nation's debt is "private," in the hands of vulture funds.)

Greek Finance Minister Varoufakis said on June 5, that Greece needs a "Speech of Hope." In 1944, there was a Morgenthau Plan to deindustrialize Germany permanently; but in 1946, U.S. Secretary of State James Byrnes gave a "Speech of Hope." You can't punish entire generations, Byrnes said. We need to rebuild Germany. The Greek Finance Minister said this is the model for today, and he invited German Chancellor Merkel to Athens to change the policy toward Greece's debt.

The Fight As Seen From Greece

by Dean Andromidas
EIR, Wiesbaden, Germany

Summary: I just spent a week in Greece, my fourth trip in five years. Up until now, it was like visiting a concentration camp—surrounded by suffering and despair. They had a Quisling government. They felt situation was hopeless. Now, it's like Stalingrad.

EIRNS/Christopher Lewis
Dean Andromidas

The suffering continues, but now they have a government elected by the population as a signal, to the Europeans, that they've had enough.

The suffering continues, but the fight is there, and this is very, very important. It is important for the people in this room, to understand what their personal responsibility should be during this period.

But just to give you some graphic idea of what the situation is like. It never ceases to amaze me—at each visit, over five years, the situation gets unbearably worse.

This new government has inherited a policy of genocide imposed by the EU institutions. It is everywhere to be seen. You read in the newspapers here that it is 27% unemployment; it is not 27%, but 45% unemployment. They don't tell you about the 300,000 small businesses which have gone bankrupt, that don't show

up on the official unemployment rolls. You have to go Athens and see all the boarded-up shops. These are the small businesses that supported families.

So we're talking about 45%. How do these people live? On the pensions of their grandparents—as many as ten people. The grandparents, their sons, their sons' families—supporting three generations in a single household. They're living on a pension of 400 euros a month; that has been cut by between 25-45%. These are the pensions Brussels wants the government not to pay this month, so that they can pay the debt. This is the situation.

The lack of certainty in the country is unbearable. I talked to normal people, taxi drivers, businessmen. There is uncertainty at all levels. The pensioner not only worries about whether he will get his pension, but whether he can pay for medications that keep him alive? The ECB [European Central Bank—ed.] is cutting off liquidity to Greece, but flooding bankrupt banks in France and Germany with it, for free. Greece gets nothing. You have to understand what it means not to have liquidity in the banking system. Viable companies in Greece, hotels, can't get simple liquidity they need for day-to-day operations. They are being told by the EU to cut wages down to 300 euros/month, to attract foreign investment. Well, foreign investment is not attracted to Greece. Who's going to go and invest in Greece now, with all this uncertainty, and the fact that the economy has collapsed?

The Athens business district—the main business district of the country—is like a needle park. We're walking the streets and we saw addicts shooting up.... The national dress is blue jeans. Not designer blue jeans. They're wearing blue jeans because they're unemployed. And not just people in the streets. In the ministries!...

Now there is resistance. This government is led by the Syriza Party, which had never won more than 4% of the vote before January. This was to give the sign to Brussels, to Berlin, etc., that the Greek people have had enough. If you look at Syriza, this is not a cocktail socialist party. They have had enough. Some left the traditional Communist Party. Some had been students who were imprisoned and tortured under the military junta. This is something unique.

Resistance
Greece has a history of 3,000 years of resistance to the Persian, Ottoman, and British Empires. You have

the ongoing war which has not ended, against the British Empire.

And you know, a lot of Greek classicists, European professors of Classical history, try to say that the population which is in Greece now has nothing to do with the ancients; even the language is not the same. If you try to tell that to a Greek now, he'll kill you. Because this is what gives them the strength.

The question of resistance is very deep. In 1942, a 16-year-old climbed the Acropolis and pulled down the Nazi flag, which started the European resistance. He is now 90, and has a seat in the European Parliament for Syriza. And that's what the nature of the resistance is. It's everyone is a resistance of people of all ages, especially retired people, who have been in government, in politics, but have not been very active before this crisis, are fighting the struggle of their lives. Many of them are in their 70s. Like former Ambassador Chrysanthopoulos, retired diplomat; he had to sell his car, he had to move out of his apartment, and move into the traditional country home; and he is fighting. And there are others. So the resistance is there.

And there is another resistance fighter, Mikos Theodorakis, and this is very important, because this tradition is what motivates people now in this fight. Now, Mikos Theodorakis is the most famous Greek modern composer. He will be celebrating his 90th birthday. He's very sick, because the wounds that he suffered, from torture when he was in the wartime [World War II—ed.] resistance, during the civil war in the '40s, during the military junta in the '60s and '70s, are finally affecting his health, and he can't be as active. But this man is a living legend, a symbol of struggle. He took the poetry of Greece's modern poets, many of them Nobel Prize winners, who lived through the civil wars and Nazi occupation and wrote very moving poems; and he put them to music, and he used this music to mobilize the population politically in '50s and '60s. And many of the young people who were part of this movement are now in this government. So the resistance is there.

A taxi driver I met said, "The government is trying." And then he said, "You know, we don't feel we are part of Europe; we feel that we own Europe. We Greeks created Europe."

That's the attitude they have. One of my friends is an engineer. All are being heavily taxed. The unborn are taxed, the unemployed are taxed, and if you have children, your tax is higher. He told me, "We engineers pay taxes"—despite the fact that many don't work, because they're supposed to be independent consultants. And many of them have tax debts. He told me, "We meet at the Engineers Association, and we discuss this crisis from the standpoint of Socrates and Plato, to apply them to understanding and fighting through this crisis."

What Can Be Done

I thought to myself, "What am I going to tell these people?... They know about the financial oligarchy.... Glass-Steagall is in their program; most people want to hang the bankers.... They have, in effect, joined the BRICS. They know this, they're acting on it."

I'm not going to tell them, "You should simply leave the euro zone." Why should Greece, the weakest of all the countries, take on the most difficult task of all? Greece is not Germany or France. It does not have the resources to take on this responsibility now. They have imports. Who is going to pay for the medicine they have to import?

I had to tell them what am I doing, what we are doing in this war. They're at the point, as they say in the military, at the front line; they have a mission, and they're carrying it out. So I brought the ideas and the analysis of Lyndon LaRouche, who has a very significant understanding of our situation now, particularly in the United States.

So in the United States, Mr. LaRouche has specifically said that we have to pass Glass-Steagall—we were the ones who started that movement—and join the BRICS, and we've been mobilizing for this. Now, we have a big break, with the former governor of Maryland Martin O'Malley campaigning for President, and Mr. LaRouche has said he's the only competent candidate at this moment, because he has made Glass-Steagall, and opposing Wall Street, the main plank of his campaign. I told them that we are not forming a vote for O'Malley campaign, but to create the presidential establishment needed now, to deal with the problems we are facing now; and that's the way to get someone with these qualifications into the White House.

I told them that Greece must act to impact this development and get this change. And once you get a change like this in the United States, we have the power to change the policy in Europe.

And those closest to the center of government understood that immediately. There is no question in their minds. "This is the way we have to act."

What have you, in this audience, done in this war, to

destroy the evil oligarchy that is responsible for what is happening in Greece, and will happen in the rest of Europe if we don't stop it? That's the way people have to think and act.

In Greece, there is a famous, beloved author named Nikos Kazantzakis. He wrote in the first half of the last century. And on his tomb, he has the inscription, "I fear nothing, I hope for nothing, therefore I am free." The point is, I act, not with a hope, necessarily, that there will be a change; but I have to act—because of my humanity. That's the attitude that many Greeks have now. And it's the attitude we have to have when we leave this room.

Our weapon is Glass-Steagall, which will destroy the financial oligarchy. Our allies are the BRICS; and our power are the ideas that we can generate to save humanity—not just at this moment, but 50, 100, 200 years from now. And that's what the Greek situation, really, is all about.

Fatal Debts Make Illusion of Independence

by Diogène Senny
Secretary General, UMOJA

To understand the problem of the fatal debt which is assailing the African Continent, it is necessary to go back to the origins and the reasons which have led to its development. Once we have shown that the African debt is a cleverly orchestrated policy of new conquest by the neo-colonial forces, it will be easy for each one of us to characterize it as being odious and illegitimate.

EIRNS/Christopher Lewis
Diogène Senny

Consequently, its cancellation is not a request for generosity from the creditors, but a reparation and an act of justice for the people betrayed.

After the accession to independence of African na-

tions in the '60s, the former colonial powers gave themselves two major tasks: Prevent by all means the rise to power in the former colonies of any regime of nationalist-panafricanist tendency; and in the context of the Cold War and with the help of the United States, prevent the Soviet Union from finding any ally in Africa, and thus gaining an access to the mineral resources, which were until then the exclusive privilege of the Western powers....

The West did everything it could to keep its hand on the former colonies. One of the weapons it would use was the debt, a pretext in official discourse for reproducing the success of the Marshall Plan to Africa, while in fact the reason was to maintain a strategic geopolitical hold and access the mineral resources as in the former colonial times....

At least three historical phenomena have provided the West the financial means to get its hold on the African Continent. First, at the time of the accession to independence, in the '60s, the western private banks disposed of huge amounts of euro-dollars. To avoid the massive return of these Euro-dollars to the United States—not only because of the strong inflation which it would induce in the U.S. economy, but also because of the risk of draining the gold detained by the United States—the western governments encouraged their banks to lend massively, at very advantageous rates, to the new and nominally independent African countries.

Naturally, the African regimes, from which the western powers had secured allegiance, showed a strong interest in these loans, in such a strong inflow of money, particularly for their own use.

The second historical phenomenon which can explain the explosion of the debt, is the oil shock of 1973, provoked by a sudden quadrupling of the oil price. The emirs of the Gulf countries would then deposit these vast quantities of dollars resulting from the profits achieved by the oil sales, within the western banks. This is the phenomenon of the so-called Petrodollars. These Petrodollars would again flock towards Africa. Hence, within a period of 20 years, from 1960 to 1980, the private part of the Third World debt exploded. From almost zero at the beginning of the 1960s, it reached $2.5 billion in 1970, and $38 billion in 1980.

Finally, the third phenomenon related to the explosion of the debt, is what we call the bound aid, coming from a bilateral source, meaning that it is granted between States directly. This bound aid is a type of indirect subsidy for the western firms whose interests are served by the African people. This practice goes back to the crisis that hit Europe in the year 1973-1975, and which is known as the end of the thirty glorious years—that is the 30 years of strong [European] growth mainly due to the capital invested within the framework of the Marshall Plan.

In fact, to find market opportunities for products which could not be sold in the Western World due to the reduction of the buying power, the idea was to grant loans to be used exclusively for the purchase of goods produced within the creditor country, even if they were more expensive or ill-adapted to the development plan of the purchasing country. From $6 billion in 1970, the bilateral aid exploded, reaching $36 billion in 1980.

The Dictators' Debts

So, dear friends, anybody who has followed closely this narrative and the reasons for the explosion of the African debt, which will prove to be fatal and deadly for the African people, will come with us to the conclusion that all these initiatives have nothing to do with the generosity and the preoccupation for the development of the Continent, the more so that the African regimes aligned with the West and other beneficiaries of these huge transfers of wealth were ostensibly despotic, corrupted and venal.

From Idi Amin Dada in Uganda, Mobutu in Zaïre, Mengistu in Ethiopia, Samuel Doe in Liberia, to Bokassa in the Central African Republic, they all competed with each other in terms of their brutality, their crazy spendings, and their total indifference towards the most elementary and fundamental needs of the population.

We can still recall that the coronation, with the approval of the Vatican, of Bokassa in 1977, a great admirer of Napoleon the First and a great friend of Giscard d'Estaing, cost one-fifth of the annual budget of the Central African Republic; that is, 22 million euros. The gigantic embezzlements of money operated by Mobutu and deposited in western banking accounts amounted to almost $8 billion, while the debt of Zaïre at the time of his fall in 1996 was standing at $12 billion.

In addition to the two debt-financing methods mentioned above, the western banks for the private part and the western states for the bilateral bound aid, we have to mention also the IMF/World Bank duo, for the multilateral part of the debt. From zero at the beginning of the 60s, the multilateral part of the African debt was standing at $1.2 billion in 1970, and $15.5 billion in 1980.

Private debt, bilateral debt, multilateral debt: all together in 1980, the African Continent was overburdened by $89 billion of debts. Africa was deprived of any viable health system, of any good infrastructure, of any educational system, and the misery was still increasing. What happened with the $89 billion borrowed by our governments? Where was the human development?

Let's recall that in 1980, the African debt was denominated in dollars, in French francs, in Deutsche marks, in Sterling pounds and in Japanese yen, which forced the Africans countries to secure strong currencies to reimburse the loans contracted.

Year in and year out, the African continent was still paying its debt. However, under the combined effect of the drop of prices of raw materials and the steep increase in interest rates on the dollar or the pound at the beginning of the '80s, the African countries, as well as the rest of the indebted Third World, found themselves incapable of reimbursing their debt. Thus was born the debt crisis, with the emergence of shock therapy and harsh medicine ordered by the IMF/World Bank, the Paris Club, the London Club and consorts....

Ending Bankers' Arithmetic

This crisis led to the strangulation of these countries, the more so because the western banks refused to grant new loans as long as the old debts were outstanding. The world was marching on its way towards a cascading debt default, of historic dimensions.

To prevent the successive bank failures that were in the making, the IMF and the industrialized countries granted new loans to keep the private banks afloat. This snowball effect consisted in contracting new loans to allow a roll-over of the old ones.

But the new loans were conditioned by the submission to structural adjustment plans, leading to the outright loss of sovereignty on economic matters....

Everything looks like the African people are forced to endure a double punishment. After having endured the torments of dictatorial regimes, they are sacrificed regularly for the sake of repaying odious and illegitimate debts, contracted by those same unjust regimes, with the complicity of shady creditors. The cynicism is reaching here its height, when the population is forced to suffer the consequences of the reimbursement of debts contracted for the purchase of military equipment, which have caused thousands of deaths in the succession of conflicts on the Continent.

According to UNCTAD, between 1970 and 2002, Africa has received $540 billion in loans. $550 billion have been repaid, but the debt is standing at $295 billion today.

According to the work of the CADTM (Committee for Abolition of Third World Debt), for Sub-Saharan Africa, the outflow of money through debt service, and the repatriation of profits from the transnational enterprises, is almost equivalent to the inflow of money related to development assistance and the sending of money by foreign workers, combined. The outflow is even $1 billion more than the inflow. In 2012, the profits returned from this region, which is the poorest in the world, amounted to 5% of its GDP, while development assistance amounted to only 1% of its GDP.

We have to ask here: who is helping whom?

That is why a civic audit of the African debt is a must.

An instrument of sovereignty, a civic audit is meant to … answer many questions. For example: Why has the government contracted a debt which is always increasing? For which political choices and which social interests has the debt been contracted? Who has benefited from it? How much interest was paid, at which rate, which portion of the capital has already been repaid? How did private debts become public ones?…

But as a political organization, our movement, the Panafrican League UMOJA, is conscious of the fact that the issue of the African debt is one that is eminently political. It is not sufficient to want or claim an audit of the debt, because one would need to create the balance of power advantageous enough to engage the African States on this road.

That is why, in front of the creditors assembled under the IMF/World Bank banner, a united front against the debt is also a Pan-African goal.

The New Suez Canal

by Prof. Mohamed Ali Ibrahim

Panel IV also included Prof. Mohamed Ali Ibrahim, Dean of the Transport and Logistics Institute, Arab League Academy of Science and Technology, Port Said, Egypt.

Due to his illness, Prof. Ibrahim's remarks were reported by his daughter, with Power Point slides.

Summary: The subject was how international financial institutions, especially the IMF and World Bank, related to the development of mega-projects like the new Suez Canal. The project includes the canal itself, and development of the surrounding area.

The project is increasing the canal's length and depth, enabling ships to sail in both directions at once; thus 97, not 49 vessels per day; and reducing waiting time. There will be six new tunnels crossing underneath the new canal, for roads and railroads.

In the logistics area around Port Said, Ismailia, Suez, there will be a buildup of industry, agriculture, communications, and tourism, which will reduce unemployment and increase living standards.

The World Bank and IMF have a conditionalities program detrimental to the developing countries—demanding that they reduce the public sector, devalue, sell off the country's assets in privatization and debt-for-equity swaps.

Egypt chose to raise the money for the new canal from its own people, and was successful. Prof. Ibrahim called on the World Bank to finance the next phase of the project.

During the discussion, Karel Vereycken of the Schiller Institute said that the World Bank should be bypassed, and called for a policy in line with the new BRICS financial institutions.

Acheikh Ibn-Oumar, former Foreign Minister of Chad, also addressed Panel IV. His speech, in French, was not available to EIR *at our press deadline.*

In addition to the listed speakers, there was a short presentation by Metin Apti, President of the Silk Road Association in Romania. The Silk Road Association is a private company, started in 2012. It's mission is to create a platform for increasing the cultural, ethnic, historical, economic, scientific, security, and spiritual connections along the Silk Road linking Asia and Europe—a fundamental connection. It promotes common projects—transportation routes, intermodal corridors. It promotes the Danube River as a corridor to ship cargo to central Europe.

Messages to the Conference From the United States

Lyndon LaRouche

I am, as you know, Lyndon LaRouche, and I'm speaking from Virginia in particular, addressing the events which are occurring in France at this time. My wife Helga has intervened to bring me into that role. We will have some other representatives, I'm sure, in France, to share this program.

The crucial issue, however, in Europe right now is the case of Germany: If the leading forces in Germany persuade Merkel, from the course she's carrying on so far, or if she agrees to accept that operation, there are forces in Germany which are now disposed to prevent any military conflict between Russia and Germany.

The particular significance of this action by Germany, is that Germany's economy has a very special value today. Despite all the problems that the German nation suffers in economic problems and so forth, Germany still has a leading validity in terms of economy in Europe. And therefore, if the German economy, the leaders of the German economy, contrary to what Merkel has been doing so far, were to exert their influence effectively, then Germany would actually take steps which would, in effect, prevent a military conflict between Europe, or specifically Germany, and Russia. That would be probably sufficient to thwart any attempt to spread a global thermonuclear war of the type that the British system, and its stooge, Obama, is pushing hard right now.

Therefore, those who are in France, or participating in the things that are going on in France now, should look carefully at this, because this is the interest of all us. Because if a general thermonuclear war were to be launched, and it would be launched under the auspices of Barack Obama, the President of the United States, then the effect would be *probably permanent*. Maybe some human beings would survive, but the system of society as we've known it heretofore, would be completely changed, and mostly obliterated.

So therefore, it's extremely important that we break the attempt to use Europe, or European nations, for their own role in their self-destruction. And the one nation which is best suited to do that, would be certain leading figures in Germany, acting simply on the basis of defending the German economy. That would be a sufficient motive to stop what Obama is doing, if the people in the United States would pick up on the same thing.

If we don't succeed in that direction, or something tantamount to that, there's no doubt, that most of the human race would disappear, and disappear very suddenly. It would not be a long war in its battle form; it would be quick, massively destructive, more destructive than anything conceived before. It would be sudden, and the planet would be finished, as far as human beings understand today.

And I'm working on that issue from here. I'm working also on trying to encourage people in other parts of the world, to recognize that, so that some of them, who have considered me to be some kind of an authority on these kinds of matters, may respond to what I'm saying. And if they do, and take the actions I've suggested,—that we take steps to make sure that Obama is blocked from launching thermonuclear war, by the British Empire but under Obama, to launch a general war which is steaming up right now,—if we stop that, we can save civilization. Otherwise, we have very poor chances.

So, that's where I think I would like to encourage those participating in the proceedings in France at this time, to put their contribution from various nations that are participating, in taking this view, that we must find, hopefully with help from leading forces in Germany, to take a step to *break the bloc* which is trying to unite all of Western Europe and beyond, into a single attack on Russia.

Russia will respond to an attack, mercilessly, and with great efficiency. But it would be a Russia virtually sacrificing its own existence, in order to bring down those parts of the planet which were trying to destroy, in particular Russia, but also civilization generally.

This British/Obama connection is the greatest threat to mankind known in history so far, and there can be no doubt, by any competent analyst, to recognize that that is the case at hand now. That the coming weeks are, as of now, unless a change occurs, the signal for the extermination of most of humanity. And that's what I'm talking about, and *I'm right*, and it's important.

Rep. Walter B. Jones

I'm Walter Jones. I represent the 3rd Congressional District of North Carolina in the United States House of Representatives, and today[1] was a special day and a day for truth and honesty and integrity in our government.

Rep. Walter B. Jones

I want to thank Sen. Rand Paul, Sen. Ron Wyden, Sen. [Kirsten] Gillibrand, for coming out and joining on the Senate side to duplicate what we've done on the House side. This has been on the House side, H.Res.14, has been the second Congress that we've introduced the bill. All it does is call on the President to please keep his word to the 9/11 families and declassify the 28 pages.

I have read the 28 pages, and the 28 pages have nothing to do with national security, *nothing*, or I wouldn't be standing here. It's all about relationships and involvement in 9/11. So for me personally, what is happening today, with the Senate taking the lead—and again, I thank Sen. Rand Paul, he mentioned today that I called him numerous times about getting involved, but we knew this would be a process. We knew it wouldn't happen in 30 days or six months. But the longer we could keep beating the drum, this was a huge drumbeat

---

1. Rep. Jones authorized the release of this statement, made on the sidelines of the June 2 press conference on the announcement of the introduction of a Senate bill calling for the release of the 28 pages, as a greeting to the Paris conference.

on the Senate side today!

We have Senator Graham, who's been so outspoken on this issue for years; then you have Senator Rand Paul and Gillibrand and Wyden who now have come together. We need to keep beating this drum. And I hope that the citizens in New York/New Jersey and all the surrounding states will get behind and encourage their delegation to join in this effort to bring peace, as much as you can, to the 9/11 families and bring the truth to the American people.

Virginia State Sen. Richard Black

I'd like to welcome all of you to the Paris conference. We are in extraordinarily perilous times, both financially and militarily. Since the Great Recession of 2007, the world has entered a period of unprecedented fiscal profligacy. This printing of money threatens the entire global financial architecture. On the military side, the United States has allowed Saudi Arabia and Turkey to lead NATO

Virginia State Sen. Richard Black

into a dangerous strategy of regime change. This has unleashed two of the most sinister terrorist armies in modern history: ISIS and the Army of Conquest. The Army of Conquest is built around Al Qaeda in Syria, the very force that attacked the United States and murdered 3,000 Americans on 9/11.

These two forces threaten the very existence of Europe. In June, Turkey's president Erdogan warned opponents that he would not let anyone extinguish the fires of conquest burning in the heart of Istanbul for 562 years. His statement celebrates one greatest war crimes in human history: the rape of Constantinople in 1453, when Turks murdered and defiled Christians in the city for weeks before selling 30,000 of the survivors into slavery. Europe must not ignore Erdogan's words and his Army of Conquest. The world must find a new paradigm. This conference provides an opportunity to find a new way, one that is urgently needed.

A New Scientific and Cultural Renaissance Is Key to Our Future

Moderator Odile Mojon opened this panel stating that it was intended to sharpen the weapons of the participants in the struggle against the criminal fraudsters of the big "climate summit" scheduled for Paris in December. Of the following four presentations, three were based heavily on visuals which are not available as of this writing, and thus will only be summarized below. They will be available on the Schiller websites as soon as possible.

Jean Jaurès: Nurturing Politics with Art and Science

by Maëlle Mercier
Schiller Institute, Paris

Good afternoon,

We are a group of young activists having studied Jean Jaurès, in order to deal with today's challenges, and from the standpoint of that decisive moment of the Twentieth Century where not only was he murdered, but where humanity fell into a new Barbary—that of the war of trenches and of ideologies.

Ladies and Gentlemen

Why have we gathered here today? What is the basis of the BRICS' drive toward a new paradigm, and of those very real infra-structural projects which are being built in the world at breathtaking speed?

It's nothing more than an idea; a very small idea which even though infinitesimal, is uplifting men, shifting mountains, and will soon change the Universe. (The New Space silk road and the lunar program!)

This idea however could have never sprung from the pragmatic "souls," from the "realistic" minds such as those of our Western leaders.

Why? Because they have been programmed to reason in terms of a given system, of its "geopolitics," its debts, its contracts, its balance of power (dominant and dominated); because they only reason in terms of what they "see," of that which exists already and that which is past.

Without imagination, without the power of mind therefore and its capacity to move beyond the present, and beyond matter, the future is condemned.

The challenge for our civilization is thus to give it back its part of the "ideal," of "infinity." This is a very difficult thing to do within the context of this materialist, violent and sexual counter-culture where man has been reduced to the state of an animal, determined by its passions and his senses.

And in particular here, in this country of Cartesian doubt which is France, where the only alternative to this bestialisation is not "the ideal," but the impotent prison of mathematical abstraction and analysis (the French are well known for their rabid criticisms, and their commentaries on reality, but they do not act)! In

EIRNS/Christopher Lewis
Maëlle Mercier

short, to give back to man its full humanity and capacity to transform and create the condition s of the future, he must bring harmony to his emotions and his reason, and recreate the faculty of imagination.

If this is the role of Art (something which Friedrich Schiller developed magnificently), of philosophy and science (Leibniz), is this something that can be realized through politics?

Yes! The proof is the philosophical struggle of Jean Jaurès who was indeed inspired by Leibniz and Schiller.

What Jaurès Fought

It is well known that Jean Jaurès was murdered for having attempted to stop World War One, that war in which the great powers ripped themselves apart because, like today, they were on the verge of forming a new alliance, a new model for peace and progress, and because the British Empire saw that process as a danger for its own power.

Indeed, France, Russia, and Germany—thanks to certain of their elites such as Gabriel Hanotaux and Sergei Witte—had laid the foundations for the new Silk Road through the construction of the Transiberian and Berlin-Bagdad railways.

Yet, dark clouds in the horizon hovered first over France, before moving onto Germany in the 1930's, and to Italy next. The same clouds of which Jaurès said: "Capitalism carries within itself the germ of war, like rain clouds carry thunder storms."

Jaurès was born in 1859, the year of the publication of "On the Origin of Species." In this essay, the British Charles Darwin developed his famous doctrine of evolution. However, is this theory of the survival of the fittest, not the perfect justification of the oligarchic principle of social triage, of which British liberalism and Malthusianism are so fond?

Just prior to that, Gobineau, a Frenchman, had published his "Essay on the Inequality of Human Races."

Jean Jaurès in 1914

Since the end of the Nineteenth Century, a fad had developed among distinguished and intellectual French circles: how to identify the "races" according to human morphological traits.

It is thus that left-wing French anthropoligist, Vacher de Lapouge, who liked to measure the skulls of men in order to justify the thesis developed in his book *The Aryan: His Social Role*, provided already then the main arguments for Nazism:

There are no more rights of men, than there are rights of the Tatou (…) or of eatable beef. There are only forces. Fraternity is all right, but woe to the losers! Life can only be maintained by death. To live one has to kill, kill in order to eat.

What are the common bases of all those doctrines which created the perfect grounds for the anti-Semitism and the anti-German revanchism which emerged in France in those years?

It was a fixed and material vision of man, defined only by his body, his organic material, his physical relations to the world, a world itself totally arbitrary: a negation thus, of the human mind, of its capacity to change, to discover, to create, a capacity for transcendence.

This situation is further aggravated by the rule of positivism, a doctrine founded by the Frenchman Auguste Comte, who chopped history into predetermined ages, negating the role of human will and of ideas. First two naïve ages : the theological age of the Middle-ages and the metaphysical age of the Renaissance; then the modern rational age: the age of positivism where a so-called science inherited from the Enlightenment, finally rules.

This objective science would have finally understood, following Newton and Descartes, that the world is totally dependent on matter: there is no sense, no

God, no unity. And being chaotic, one cannot apprehend it except by approximation, only relying on facts accumulated through our sense perception.

In short, since ideas do not exist, and since one cannot have access to the causes of things, one is incapable of any discovery (not even that of universal gravitation, by nature invisible to our sense). And, one cannot change the world.

The working-class parties and the political entourage of Jaurès, will be deeply hampered by this: Incredible, for revolutionary left wing parties!

For Jules Ferry, for instance, whom France celebrates for his defense of a secular education:

> One does not revolt against what is; one does not substitute, in social practice, what could be to what there is. The concentration of capitals is a certain fact . . .; one does not engage against this general tendency which operates like a mechanical force, an impossible and ridiculous struggle. (*The Positive Philosophy*, 1867)

The Marxists were in a comparable situation: Since they defend a materialist conception of history, having, according to them, its own internal logic, they de facto condemn the individual and the proletariat to be nothing but objects of forces and of a class struggle which transcends them.

In those conditions, progress is both impossible and fiercely rejected, to such an extent that in 1911, those close to Maurras, an extreme right-wing nationalist, and George Sorel, a self-defined Marxist, said that in France:

> In order to save civilization, the first animal to kill is the belief in progress, it is that optimism . . . which generated the sinister farce of the [French revolution] of 1789.

It is difficult, in those conditions to envisage any other solution than that of all against all, the struggle for a vital space! Something which should make us reflect upon those politically correct myths circulating today, which negate the creation of new resources and promote theories of de-growth and of green energies.

It is thus in the name of progress and to give back to the world and to man, their right to infinity, their right to create and to generate ideas to insure the future, that Jaurès led his political and philosophical struggle against the beginnings of fascism.

'An Acting Infinite'

Jaurès' doctoral dissertation, "On the reality of a sensuous world," prepared under the direction of a Leibnizian philosopher, attacked the positivists and materialists, but also the "idealists" and the "formalists" for being just as dangerous. He scored the idealists for condemning reality as a vain illusion, and the formalists, for reducing it to the "dryness of a logical construction."

His aim was to show the scientific, rather than the ideological, character of progress, as an integral part of nature and of human nature. He proved that there is a permanent interaction between the living and the thinking, between ideas and things, allowing the constant creation of increasingly superior forms of existence.

Thus for Jaurès:

> For all the living, the problem of the infinite is fully posed, at whatever the period of the Universe they emerged."... "The sum of the movements in the world is an acting infinite, where Mathematics does not have its place. One should not consider the Universe, and its movements and energies, as an unending budget . . . . Here, it is not the resources that measure the expenses; it is rather the infinity of the work to be accomplished which provides for a correspondent infinity of resources.

The above is an appropriate attack on the partisans of budget austerity ruling today in Washington and in Brussels.

This is fully coherent with his political and parliamentary struggle according to which:

> every individual has the right to full growth. He has thus the right to demand from humanity all that can second this effort(*Socialism and Life*).

And indeed, Jaurès will defend, against capitalism and usury, the idea of national credit, of a public bank issuing currency to service the future productive needs of the nation, which will be finally realized during the Thirty glorious years after WWII.

Let us reflect upon this passage of his thesis, which is very polemical from a philosophical standpoint, but fundamental. It is after the beginning of chapter 3, when after having descended layer by layer, from molecules to the small atoms, in the infinitely small of matter, he concludes:

> Science itself, when seeking for the support of material movement and for the last element of matter, leads us to a reality which has nothing material left to it, which cannot be perceived by the senses, which only exists for the mind.

Comparing his exploration to that of Virgil and Dante, who, having taken another road to leave the depth of Inferno, finally rediscovered the stars . . . Jaurès continues:

> Guided by science, we continued to descend always further, always lower in the depth of matter; and there also, in those dangerous abysses where one could wonder whether all would not dissolve in blind fatality, we found movements superposed, circles and whirlpools: and at the opposite opening of those abysses, we also rediscovered the stars.

Mind is the Basis for Matter

Let me now make a detour to the great physicist Max Planck to whom we owe the discovery of the quantum. This is what he declared at the end of his life in the 1930s, as the materialist and utilitarian conception of man was coming to its apogee in Germany, with the horrors that were experienced there:

> As a physicist who committed his entire life to a sober science, the study of matter, I am surely free of any suspicion that could make of me a fanatic. And so I affirm on the basis of my research on the atom, that there is no matter in itself. All matter does not emerge or exist except for a force which sets in motion the atomic and keeps them together like the most minute solar systems of the Universe. But since there is neither intelligent force, nor any exterior force in the Universe as a whole, we must postulate an intelligent mind behind this force. Mind is thus the basis for matter.

Indeed, if one reflects upon this well, a paradox surrounds us permanently, and it's something that Jaurès will not hesitate to use during a debate against Marx's son-in-law, Paul Lafargues, a debate published under the heading of "Materialism and idealism in the conception of history."

How can our brain itself generate new ideas, new scientific discoveries, if the origin of those ideas was not to be found in the mechanical cogs of matter, chemical reaction after chemical reaction?

Jaurès responded:

> If I'm saying these words at this moment, it's because the idea that I am expressing at this very minute arose lengthily from a prior idea and from the series of all prior ideas. But it is also because I want to realize in the future what I see before me, an aim, an intention, an end; and thus my present thought, while it seems to be determined by the series of past thoughts, has been also provoked by an idea of the future. Yet it is the same with history: while one can explain all the historical phenomena by pure economic evolution, you can also explain them by the restless and permanent desire of humanity of a higher form of existence. Before the experience of history, before the constitution of such or such economic system, humanity carries in itself a pre-established idea of justice and of right and it is this preconceived ideal that it pursues from a form of civilization to a superior form of civilization.

Ideas are not social conventions, pure inventions of the brain, or of human society. They are not detached entities from the real world. They are "natural" in the sense that the Universe, for its own needs, to continue its task of creation of the world, generates them through the human mind.

Yet, what is this idea that is at the foundation of the BRICS movement and the New Silk Road? This idea is that of progress, progress to go beyond the borders of the unknown. And how will it be ensured? By mutually assured creativity and human discovery.

We absolutely need to win the struggle of Jaurès. If not, once again humanity will be destroyed, and with it, the world.

Water, An Unlimited Resource Provided We Understand Where It Comes From

by Benjamin Deniston

Deniston began by warning that the planned Paris "climate summit" is about imposing total control on the world's energy consumption. It is a project driven by pure racist ideology, as exemplified by Prince Philip who is so hateful of mankind that he wants to be reborn as a deadly virus to help reduce "overpopulation." Contrary to what Prince Philip and other such people want to make people believe, there is no such thing as limited resources, nor any limits to human creativity and an intervention into nature, Deniston said, taking the example of water, scarcity of which in California has been taken as pretext for massive media propaganda against population growth.

Water is more than just the water that is visibly there; it can be generated by man through desalination, or better by ionization—no animal could ever do that. Water is linked to Galactic cycles, its generation by nature has to do with the Solar System's cycle through the different sections of the Galaxy, which produces variations in atmospheric radiation. That much is known, and experiments with generating water through devices producing ions, have been carried out in numerous countries or are still being carried out, with first positive results. But still, many processes in the universe are not understood on the basis of means available—new hypotheses have to come in to solve unanswered questions.

The Innocence of Carbon

by Prof. François Gervais

Prof. Gervais used numerous slides, showing how absurd the ecologist propaganda is on the climate issue:

There is, as shown in many scientific papers to which the IPCC never paid any attention, no indication of a connection between rising CO_2 and rising temperatures. There is, however, a connection between Sun cycles and temperature rise, and whereas CO_2 has increased during the recent years, we even observe a decrease in average temperatures. We are even facing a temperature minimum by 2078, and therefore the IPCC is dead wrong in predicting a deadly increase by 2100.

But these things happen if people do not know the simple difference between a thermometer and a barometer: The latter, invented by Toricelli 300 years ago, shows that air pressure gives you an indication of the weather. The thermometer gives you the temperature, but it will not tell you about the weather. When the IPCC blames all weather changes on temperature rises and "man-made climate changes," it is simply wrong. These alleged scientists should not be believed, Gervais concluded.

The Deception of Climatic Warming

by Prof. Carl-Otto Weiss (Emeritus)

Prof. Weiss said that only after his retirement did he have time to deal with the IPCC issue, and in doing intense private research in collaboration with some astronomers, he found evidence that all climate change of the past centuries was due to natural cycles.

Weiss showed slides demonstrating that if such natural cycles are superimposed on curves of temperature increases, there is a striking congruence, with no man-made aspect in it. And changes in temperature are only occurring in congruence with cycles. If man were responsible, the rise would be constant in the way the IPCC argues. And as concerns CO_2, most of it is absorbed by the biosphere and the oceans in particular, and never reaches the atmosphere. Extreme weather as discovered by the IPCC, has not increased, because, among other reasons, rising temperature makes the weather less violent.

Finally, Weiss said, CO_2 is good for plants, and thus for all life on this planet; the crop yield is increased, and so is forest growth. CO_2, which the greenies want to eliminate, is as a matter of fact leading to a substantial greening of deserts, Weiss concluded.

Create a New Renaissance

by Helga Zepp-LaRouche

Well, I would like to go into the matter of culture, but unfortunately, I have to go first into the area of counter-culture. That is, in commenting on this last panel, I was very, very shocked—and, as a matter of fact, it really shows that we are in a war, a war for civilization,—because it was just revealed that the new Papal Encyclical, which is supposed to come out on the 18th of June, in a couple of days, will be on climate change. And if you look at who will be the presenters, the official presenters of that Encyclical, it will be Cardinal Peter Turkson, who is the head of Justicia et Pax, and it will be Metropolitan John Zizioulas of Pergamon, a leading representative of the Orthodox Church of Greece. And it will be our old acquaintance, whom I just accidentally mentioned yesterday in my speech, John Schellnhuber.

Now, this is really incredible, because, as Ben Deniston mentioned in his remarks earlier, evil is really situated in this ideology. Now, that means, the devil is about to take over the Catholic Church. Or has already taken over. They are trying to compete for evil with the Protestant Church in this respect.

Now that is a declaration of war, because they have said that they want to influence two major conferences: one is the International Conference on Financing for Development, which will take place in Addis Ababa, which means that they want to completely influence that conference, so that only "sustainable technology," only "appropriate technology" is permitted.

Hell, also known as "The Garden of Earthly Delights," by Hieronymous Bosch, created in 1503-4.

Unacceptable Horror

You have to understand that our fight against that goes back forty years or more. Because we had a positive conception—I mean, I joined this organization, because when I went on this trip in 1971, on a cargo ship which went to Africa, and parts of Asia, to Malaysia, Thailand, China, in the middle of the Cultural Revolution. But also, I could spend a couple of days in some cities of Africa. And I spent some longer time in China.

I came back from that trip, with—I mean, I really was absolutely convinced that the world could not be like that. It could not remain like that.

Because if you travel on a cargo ship, you get a completely different picture, than if you go on a cruise-liner, a luxury ship,—or if you have your well-to-do life, and you jet-set around the globe, and you go from four-star hotel, five-star hotel to five-star hotel; you don't see this. And if you belong to a certain layer in society, you blind yourself to the real condition of where mankind is.

But when you travel on a cargo ship, you see the world as it is. For instance, in Dakar, Senegal, I left the ship in the morning, at six o'clock, and there were twenty people—beautiful tall, great Senegalese women and men, who were taller than even me, and they tried to sell me some handicrafts. And I told them, look, I don't have money. I'm a student. I cannot buy this. And I could not convince them that it was futile. And I thought, what does this do to the dignity of man, if adult people feel that they have to run after me, a poor student? I knew that I couldn't get it across to them.

Then, I went—we went to Thailand. At the port, parents brought their 10, 11 and 12-year children as prostitutes for the sailors. The parents brought them.

I could go on and on. When you see what poverty does to people, in their desperation, you understand that poverty is the biggest human rights violation there is.

And therefore, I joined this organization, because when I met Mr. LaRouche, and he had these ideas that you have to develop the developing countries. We started to make plans for Africa—the first book on the development of Africa, we published in 1976. Actually, we had here in Paris, a presentation of that plan, which, it is very clear, still is needed. You need ports. You need bridges. You need roads, railway. You need infrastructure, because without infrastructure, you don't even have agriculture, because you can't transport whatever is being produced. You need food processing.

And it would be so easy to do all of this, if there were the political will.

The Four Horsemen

So anyway, now we are here so much later. But, this has been a war between our organization and like-minded people, like Indira Ghandi, with whom we worked on a forty-year development plan for India. We worked with Lopez Portillo on a development plan for Latin America, which he started to implement. And it would have succeeded if, at that time, Argentina and Brazil had cooperated.

Then in 1974, I went to the U.N. Population Conference in Bucharest, and I went there with a development plan, which was essentially the idea that you need a large-scale technology transfer from the industrialized countries to the developing sector. And it would have been very easy to overcome the underdevelopment.

But what happened, is that you had John D. Rockefeller the Third, who presented his plan, which essentially was the first time they used this terminology: sustainable development, appropriate technology. Appropriate technology means, the Africans should never get railways, they should have little shovels, and little fountains in their village. And do things that are appropriate to them.

So at that time, these ideas were new. Environmentalism was really not yet existent. And all the left groups who were at this Bucharest population conference, they said, "Oh, population explosion." Rockefeller said, there is an explosion of population. We have to reduce population. And all the left groups said, "Oh, the population bomb is a Rockefeller baby," because people knew that that was an oligarchical interest.

And I intervened at that conference. I said, look, the consequence of what you are proposing is a hundred times worse than Adolf Hitler.

Now, that was absolutely true, because, if you count the number of people who have died as a consequence of the denial of technology through imposing IMF conditionalities on the Third World, I once calculated that you come to hundreds of millions of people. And, in a certain sense, we now have a situation, where Schellnhuber, who is a CBE—Commander of the British Empire—is a complete fraudster. He's psychologically a very difficult person, to use diplomatic language. But, that he is now influencing the Catholic Church for a decarbonization of the world economy—I mean, we fought this, when he presented it to the German government, because it would mean eliminating every fossil fuel. It would mean eliminating, naturally, nuclear energy altogether.

And if you only go by renewable energies—wind, solar and so forth— you end up with the population carrying capacity of the Earth of about one billion people.

And we have studied the Zero-Growth movement way back into the early seventies, and there were people who said, "Well, how do you reduce population?" Well,

Dante Alighieri, as portrayed by Domenico di Michelino. Initiator of the Italian Renaissance.

there are the four riders, the Four Horsemen of the Apocalypse: War, Death, Famine, Epidemics, and you just let these things grow, and then the population falls by itself.

Now, if they were to succeed in imposing that into the Paris climate conference, which I don't think will happen,—but, there will be a massive attempt to do that,—it will be tantamount to really turning these institutions into genocidalist institutions. And we really have to fight against that, with all possible means. Because this is a form of Nazism, or fascism. It's eco-fascism, or, I don't know how you call it, but it's really that.

It Starts With the Mind

And so, I think that we have to really mobilize in all countries around the world to block that. And I think the panel this afternoon gave us excellent ammunition. These are fraudsters. They are, the kinds of scientists—

I don't know if you remember this old record, where you had a little dog, and a grammophone—they sing the song of whoever feeds them. These are not scientists.

This goes back to how they tried to destroy the influence of Leibniz in the Berlin Academy. They would have contests in which the most corrupt scientists would be promoted. And people like Kaestner and Lessing, and so forth—they fought against these people. This is an old trick by the oligarchy. And right now, you have a situation where many of these scientists are bored. They are not scientists; they are just doing what you get a grant for. And some of the better scientists even use green terminology, in order to get better funding. And then they sneak in their little project, so that they can do some research. But they give it a green name to get the funding.

I mean, the corruption of the mind is incredible.

Why do you think that this whole thing functions? Why do you think we are on the verge of war? Because people are too stupid to think things through, and they belong to clubs where it is the peer belief to not think that way. If you are a part of a club which is pro-British, or pro-American, then you don't even think that it could be different.

And I can only challenge you, if you have any doubts about what has been said here, that we are on the verge of World War Three,—if you have any respect for your mind, you do not just reject it. You go home and you do your homework. Because if you have not yet studied it, and come to that conclusion yourself, you are just intellectually lazy. Because I have done the work. I have looked at all the papers of all the military experts in America, in Great Britain, in Germany, in France, in Italy, in Russia, in China, and there is no question, that, if you look at the evolution of the military doctrine, if you look at the whole forward deployment, if you look at the whole first-strike doctrine, if you look at the Russian reactions, at the Chinese reactions, if you don't come to the conclusion that we are on the verge of World War Three—I hate to say it—you are an intellectual lazy bum. Or worse.

Because, if you are serious, you have to come to that conclusion. If you come to that conclusion, you have to get off your behind. because you have to do something to help to save civilization. And I think the corruption of the mind comes mainly from that fact. We're not promoting anybody's cause.

Gifts for the Future

I really think we are the only organization which takes the future into account, a thousand years from now. I even would say, a couple of billions of years from now, because I want humanity to be the immortal species. I have some good contacts who are geophysi-

Zhu Xi (1130-1200), a leading mind of the Chinese Song Dynasty's Renaissance of Confucianism.

cists. And they tell me, the human race will disappear one second after twelve, or after midnight. And I do not accept that.

Because for me—I don't know if you remember, but when the Voyager left our solar system a couple of months ago, they had records on the spaceship of Furtwängler conducting Beethoven's Ninth Symphony. So Furtwängler conducting the Ninth Symphony is now travelling outside of our solar system, which for me, is a very intriguing idea, that if there are some intelligent people somewhere—we don't know, because the universe is really big, and we only know a very tiny part of it—it could be that somebody gets this record, and listens to Furtwängler conducting the Ninth Symphony!

But the idea, that all of that would have been for nothing, all the great struggles of mankind. The Indian people, freeing themselves from British imperialism,—Mahatma Ghandi, other struggles. The Chinese liberating themselves from the Opium War. All the many, many courageous people. The German Resistance who tried to fight Hitler, and who got chopped off. All the beautiful human activities which led to the point where we are here today, would have been for nothing?

I think that that is a completely unacceptable idea. And in the spirit in which Schiller wrote "Why We Should Study Universal History," I think that we should have gratitude for the rich donations from previous generations, and organize our life in such a way that we give it richer to the future generations.

And, I think that this is really something that I want to put into your heart and into your mind. Don't think narrowly. Because it is the narrowness of the mind, which has led to two world wars. And we have set out explicitly with the idea that we must overcome geopolitical thinking, because geopolitics has twice led to world war in the Twentieth Century. And because of the existence of thermonuclear weapons, if we don't get over geopolitics right now, the danger is that we will extinguish ourwelves.

And, why did I mention yesterday in my remarks, the difference beween *ratio* and intellect? And I really want you to think about it, because most people think, "Ya, it's my *Menschenverstand*—my common sense: I know everything myself. I am a learned man. I have studied. I have titles of all kinds." But they are not self-conscious—that's what happens if they're thinking on the level of *ratio*, which is, you think in terms of contradictions. You think that my interest is against that interest. That I have this interest against the other person's. And what's the difference if you think on the level of reason or as Cusanus calls it, the level of intellect? Then you think on the level of *coincidentia oppositorum*—the coincidence of opposites, which is an idea of looking through, or you look on the level where the contradictions no longer exist. And in the philosophy of the Platonic humanist tradition of Europe, it's the idea that the One has a higher order, and a higher power, than the Many.

And you have to think in this way. Because as long as you remain on the level of contradictions, you can't solve any problem. I mean, that was the great achievement of the Peace of Westphalia. Because they recognized, that after 150 years of religious war in Europe,—if they had continued, nobody would have been left. Because in some areas of Europe, two-thirds of humanity were already destroyed. So they came to the conclusion that a higher principle had to be found. The idea of the "interest of the other." That a permanent peace can only be built on the interest of the other.

Beauty is Lawful

And that is a method of thinking which you can apply to every field. You will not make a new discovery in science if you can't hypothesize, what is the necessary step in the unknown. Scientific discovery is not that somebody has a bright idea, and then you discover something. No, it is the accumulation of knowledge, of *Geistesmassen* [thought-objects],—more Geistesmassen accumulate and resonate, and then out of that, is the necessary next step of discovery. Like, why, for example, thermonuclear fusion is one of the absolutely necessary next steps, because it leads to a higher energy-flux density, which is important for the continued existence of mankind.

In the same way, you cannot make a great composition in classical music, if you throw out all the laws of

Indian Classical poet Rabindranath Tagore, in a photo taken by Albert Kahn in 1921.

composition. Then you end up with atonal music, or with twelve-tone music, and you end up with ugliness.

You have to go through the late string quartets of Beethoven, through the beautiful symphonies, through Brahms, through Schubert, through the beautiful songs of Schubert, and all the high points of Classical music, and then define what is the next step of the composition. You have to respect the rules and enlarge the rules in a lawful way.

And in that sense, I think that mankind has reached a point where I don't think we will get out of this mess otherwise. And we have a mess. If you don't think that we are at a civilizational breakdown crisis, wake up!

I mean, look, for example, some countries have young people. Like Modi. Modi said, the reason why India has such a beautiful future is because they have so many young people. And if these young people get educated, they will be the biggest export possibility, because there are countries which have demographical crises, like Germany, Italy. These countries will vanish without the Indians in the future. Because people don't procreate anymore. I don't know, you have too many marriages of all kinds of forms which don't procreate.

So sooner or later, they will cease to exist. But fortunately, we have the Indians to help the Germans to survive. [Laughter, applause].

So,—but Modi said, if we educate these young people, then they are the potential of the future. And that is really how we have to think. Because, in a certain sense, the civilizational crisis is not just that we are on the verge of World War Three; that we have a refugee crisis which is heartbreaking. If you look at those pictures in the Mediterranean, I think that this is the declaration of bankruptcy of the EU. Because this is the worst of the worst behavior. Instead of developing Africa, they shoot at the boats. What is that? What is the self-image of the EU?

But it's not just that. It's not just that two billion people go hungry every day. Two billion people! One billion are really starving, and one billion are at the edge of not having enough to eat. And it is not necessary. It's not only that. The drugs. Look at the drugs— how many people are taking drugs. In Russia alone, every year, 40,000 people die of drugs. And Russia has said that this is the biggest national security crisis they have. Look at the young people who go to discos. Eighty-five percent of all young people going to discos take drugs! Look at the pornography. I mean, there is no limit any more. There is no longer anything that you cannot see on public television. Every time I turn on the television, which happens once in a while, I am absolutely shocked! I don't want to go through the gory details, but, I said, this cannot be. Every time that I think it has reached the absolute bottom of perversity, of pornography, of violence,—they come up with something new.

And, if you look at the youth culture, the youth culture where eight-year, nine-year, ten-year old girls and boys know everything. About sex, about homosexuality, about sexual practices, about violence, about snuff movies. Look at the British crown. Look at what happens now with the paedophilia scandal in Great Britain. This involves the top elite in Great Britain. Sir Leon Brittan, whom I had the misfortune to meet at this 1996 conference in Beijing, because he was one of the speakers. And he said, "Oh, the Silk Road will never function. Terrorism, destabilizations in all of Central Asia." And it was very clear the British Great Game does want this development.

Now, this guy is now,—he is dead. He's probably roasting in Hell already. But he was involved in the highest-level paedophilia, running boys' houses, which is huge. It involves thousands and thousands of the British elites. They're degenerates!

If you look at the total picture of the youth culture in Europe and in the United States. In the United States, you better don't go shopping, because if you go in a mall you have a good chance you will be shot, by somebody just driving by. If you look at the death rate in major cities in the United States. If you look at the police violence, why do you think in all of these cities— Ferguson, Baltimore—why do you have these riots? Because the police in the United States has been militarized. They get the heavy weapons from the Army to use against their own population. And if there is a collapse of the financial system, I think that the United States will explode in a civil war. Because you have these weapons everywhere. You have violence in the culture, which is really big. And you have now a counter-movement, in which the reverends unite in all of the United States, and they say, we have to get in the act, to prevent this from happening again.

A Qualitative Leap

So, I could go on for a long time. But if you are not blind to what is around you, you see that we are not just in a war danger, in a breakdown crisis, but we have a civilizational crisis,—like the caste system in India. There are people who think that the lower castes are lower people. And I have many good friends in India, and I have seen how they behave. I have a good acquaintance, and I saw how he behaved towards somebody who brought in the luggage in the hotel. This is oligarchical thinking. This person in India is not one iota better than the Queen running drugs. And the Queen does run drugs. We have been accused of having said that; we have proven the case.

If you look at the British-Saudi running of terrorism, which is what the issue of the "28 pages" is all about, and you heard Walter Jones, that there is a growing movement in the United States, and the truth will come out about all of this.

Anyway, I want to make the point, we have a civilizational crisis, which is really all-encompassing. And we have reached in the history of mankind, a point where either we make a qualitative jump into a completely new paradigm—and a new paradigm—there are examples in history where you can study it. Where you had a breakdown crisis, as in the Fourteenth Century in Italy, or in most of Europe actually. You had the Black Death. You had the flagellants. You had witch-burning.

You had a complete, complete collapse of society, and a collapse of the financial system. If you look at the pictures of Bosch and Breughel, where people— [groan]—one eye is going up, the other one is going down. Breughel and Bush— Bosch! [Laughter] Here you had another one of these strange-looking people! What these painters captured was the mental breakdown of society in a Dark Age.

And then you have to look at how did we manage to get into the Golden Age of the Italian Renaissance? It happened through many steps. It happened through Dante, Dante Alighieri. It happened through Petrarch, and a whole movement of humanists, who started to collect the manuscripts of great thinkers of the past. And then you had the courageous fight of Jean D'Arc, which, together with Louis XI, transformed France. The living standard of the French population doubled in twenty years during the reign of Louis XI. Then you had especially Nicholas of Cusa, and the people he influenced. He was consciously saying, we need a completely new thinking. He attacked the Scholastics. He attacked the Peripatetics—the Aristotelians who had dominated all of the universities of Europe at that time. And he developed a new method of thinking, which was the basis of the modern nation state, which was the basis of modern science. Kepler could not have done what he did without Cusa, and he always talked about the divine Cusanus.

Vernadsky talked about the great stepping-stone of Cusansky [Cusa]. And fortunately, Vernadsky is much more known in Russia than in Europe, because this is very good capital which Russia is using, or has used.

So we need a break like that. We need to have a completely new thinking, not defined from the present conflicts among nations, among ethnic conflicts, geographical conflicts—all of that, but we have to define mankind

The great Russian poet and novelist Alexander Pushkin.

as one, and think how do we survive as a human species in the future. And, if you start to define everything from that standpoint, every conflict can be solved.

We have said many times, we do not just need a new world economic order—which we have presented with the idea of a world land-bridge, as a good approximation of what that could look like,—but we need a cultural Renaissance. Because the degenerate cultures has to go. And I believe that Confucius and Lessing were completely right when they said, if you decide to become good, you can decide it. If you can decide to be loving, you can start to love. It's a moral question. Can you do it?

A Classical Revival

In the same way, I think we can break with the general culture, and I think that if each country develops their own high culture, like Germany should obviously revive the German classical period, the music from Bach, Mozart, Haydn, Schubert, Schumann, Beethoven, Brahms, and even some songs of Hugo Wolf—I want to put effort into this, and I even got my husband to agree with me. And naturally, Schiller and other great poets.

In France, you have to revive the École Polytechnique. You have to become again a science-driver society, in the tradition of de Gaulle's thinking of France having a mission. Italy has so many rich scientists and artists—Verdi, Dante, Leonardo da Vinci. India is a country which has 5,000 years of history. You have to revive the Vedic writings. The Gupta period of drama. The Indian Renaissance of the late Nineteenth to the mid-Twentieth century, where you had so many beautiful poets and thinkers—Tagore, Shri Aurobindo, Vivekananda and many others. China is on the best way with Confucius.

The United States. The United States is struggling right now to revive the better part of its history, because

German Classical musician Franz Schubert.

the United States is not a monolithic monster, or a superpower you have to be a slave to,—or just like,—because they are the most powerful. No, the United States has two fundamentally different traditions. We just had a conference in New York last weekend where the thesis, the historical research was presented that the real making of America was the overcoming of slavery. It was really the question, which of the Founding Fathers would be the dominant. Was it the ones who would fight slavery? Or was it the compromisers, who were really influenced by the British Empire? And the British Empire never agreed to have lost the greatest colony, or the most important colony from their standpoint. So they tried to subvert it.

First, through wars—the British were allied with the Confederacy. The plantation owners financed the Confederacy. Then they realized that they could not regain America through military means, and they started using other means, like the Roundtable of Lord Milner and others, Milner's Kindergarten. And the idea was that you have to convince the American establishment to run the world as an empire, based on the British Empire.

And that's the problem with the Bushes and the Obamas, because that is their philosophy right now.

But there is another America. The America of Benjamin Franklin, of Alexander Hamilton, of John Quincy Adams. Of Lincoln, of McKinley, of Franklin D. Roosevelt, of John F. Kennedy. We are right now very, very far advanced to regain that America. It's my deepest conviction, that without that, there will be no solution to the world's problems. And fortunately, you have right now a growing movement of Democrats and even a couple of Republicans, as you saw in the person of Walter Jones, you have Republicans who are absolutely decent human beings. As a matter of fact, I wish we had in Germany only one Member of Parliament like Walter Jones. Because he is a man of integrity. He is completely devoted to his constituency. There is not one wrong bone in him. And you have others like that.

So, America must become a Republic again. It must have a foreign policy like that of John Quincy Adams, who said, we have to have an alliance of perfectly sovereign republics. And that is what has to be, and then there is no problem in the world, because with that, everybody will be happy.

So I could probably find in every nation, its glorious period. But, you all know this yourselves. And you have to get to the high points of each nation and each culture. And we have to revive that. Then, out of that, we will create a new Renaissance. It will be like other Renaissances, in that you will revive what was beautiful in the past, but then, that will be the nourishment to create something even more beautiful for the future.

So I think that is the task we have immediately ahead of us. And I want you all to join in that, because this could be the most noble mission in your life. And it is necessary.

'What Man Has Never Achieved Before, Must Now Be Achieved'

This discussion took place between Lyndon LaRouche and hundreds of political activists from across the United States, on the LaRouchePAC activists' conference call June 11, 2015. John Ascher was the host.

John Ascher: This is our fourth discussion with Mr. LaRouche on the LaRouche PAC activists' conference call. Lyn, do you want to make any preliminary remarks before we take questions?

Lyndon LaRouche: Well, I think a general observation is sufficient. We have gone for four rounds now, and we're getting a very significant development, expansion, broadening of what we're doing, and this is all very good. And I think we're getting also into new territories in terms of subject matters. Probably I think there's a music theme coming in, a voice matter, or things like that. So I would not be surprised to see some novelty, relative to previous experience coming into play here.

EIRNS/Philip Ulanowsky

A science class taught in Northern Virginia in July 1986 by leading U.S. scientist Dr. Robert Moon.

Reviving Our Educational System

Ascher: Okay, so we'll begin with our first question.

Q: This is L— from Northfield, Michigan, just outside of Detroit. And it's very good to be talking to Mr. LaRouche this evening. My daughter has just finished eighth grade, and it's been an especially frustrating year with the public school American history teaching, and they're teaching my daughter all about global warming... And she plays cello, and they will not even talk about getting an orchestra in our district. ... I want to get Mr. LaRouche's thoughts on what we can do to reverse this cultural deficiency in our schools.

LaRouche: I think the appropriate kinds of education for younger children, for example, but for children generally, is not doing anything that's popularly done now. I think that only a few people in the total population have children who really are trained and developed, in order to deal with the challenges that the process of education is supposed to bring out. This is sort of a criminal thing that's being done in the educational system generally, and if a parent has the good fortune to have a child who really is up in standard, by what we used to call standard, that is almost a miracle.

Obviously, our intention must be to correct that problem. We need to have a revision of the general process of education of children, in all integrals: I mean, you've got the young ones, you've got those in middle age as youth, and you have the ones who are, say, graduating from college; these are all distinct in their behavior, and they're also distinct because of history. That is, in each of these cases, in which you start from a very young child, who is going to some kind of schooling, and then going to one who's entering a university or something like that, you find that the quality of the students' education is deteriorating generally. With each generation of children, and young people—with very rare exceptions, which are fortunate—the problem stinks.

And that means that the problem has to be addressed on a general scale. There are ways of getting at this problem, but they're not the customary ways which are practiced in most educational institutions. We certainly need a program of education, which brings these young people up to the level of the ability, which they need for future life.

Q2: Hello, this is T— from New York. I'm delighted about the opportunity to ask you this question, because I'm on the trail of scholarly justification for Bach's championing of the [A]430 Hertz as the ideal tuning pitch. Years ago, I read that [Johann Sebastian] Bach and [Johann Joachim] Quantz, both advocated 430, but I haven't been able to find the scholarly sources to demonstrate this. Could you give me an idea of where to look?

LaRouche: We have based essentially around Manhattan, a program which is coming into shape, which includes people who are not fully developed, and some people who are fully developed, and the choral supervision is excellent. And we're getting progress, and we're practicing it in the City of New York. That's our best spot right now, and I think it's easy to understand from your experience, exactly how that works: that New York is the actual, intellectual center of culture in the United States. There are exceptions to that case, but in general, you can say that New York City is the center of human culture in the United States.

And we need a program which studies the best work coming out of New York as such, in education, and then we have to see what the problems are in the New York educational process, in order to perfect it.

Ascher: Lyn, he was also specifically referring to the question of the lower tuning, which I know that you

have heard, there's been quite a bit of stir around that recently in our activities in New York.

LaRouche: And that has been one of my war-making activities, in most of my life. I've always been on that. I understood it. It came partly because my parents and other relatives were musicians, more or less qualified; my father, for example, had an excellent tenor voice and was a trained one. And my Scottish grandfather also had an excellent bass voice, so in the family, we did have some understanding.

And around the friends I had who were musicians, are musicians today, who were professional in this matter, with their help and with the help of great musicians who I've been able to work with, like the case of Norbert Brainin, who was really an exemplary figure in our time, now long since deceased.

But we do have resources, to which we can search out and gain the kind of musical program and musical training which is required for the development of the mental powers of the individual citizen, young and old alike.

Focus on the Culture

Q3: My name is F— and I'm from Detroit, Michigan. I've had the opportunity to talk with you when you were in Metro Airports back before the first Gulf War, and I asked you a question about Iraq at the time. It's very nice to hear you again, sir.

My question is this, when I talk to people who are unfamiliar with the material that the organization has put out, when I mention the British Empire, I get people staring back at me like "What? Weren't they gone?" [LaRouche laughs] So they want substantiation that this is truly an existing force that still is out there, still doing things. What would I say, to address that, as a sort of introductory question, for example?

LaRouche: Well, you know, I'm very much steeped in that concern, in particular, for various reasons because of my international activities. You know, I've been working in various countries in the planet, more or less, and so therefore, I've come into much of this thing, and I have experience from that standpoint which is relevant.

The British problem is a complicated one, but it's also essentially an evil one. That is, there are people in the British Isles and so forth, who have all kinds of variegated types of skills, some virtuous and some less so, and some rotten, some evil. And generally, we can, from experience, I, or people with my degree of experi-

Violinist Norbert Brainin, former primarius of the Amadeus Quartet, practices for a concert in honor of Lyndon LaRouche, December 2, 1988.

ence, can pick up what the different types are, of these British cultures. And most of them are impaired.

For example, this goes to the Scottish; I have a Scottish family background among other things, and you can tell the difference in the British Isles, who, in different parts of the British Isles, responds in particular, to their local cultures or their special kinds of cultures. And then you find that most of them can be very useful, can have even noble intentions. But I wouldn't like to say that the British Monarchy or the British imperial powers, are anything but evil.

Q4: D— from Metro Phoenix. A few sessions ago, you spoke about Albert Einstein, and what you thought about him, and I was going ask a question but didn't have the opportunity, to ask you what you thought about Nicola Tesla, and his contributions to science?

LaRouche: Well, this is an interesting question because it has variegated aspects to it. Some of it is significant, and the attempt to sort out the implications to various approaches to this question, is an important question in itself. Einstein, for me, is particularly important, because he was the only scientist, during the period of the Twentieth Century, who was actually competent in science. You had other people who had skills in science, and I've known some of them who have had a great degree of skill in science. But Einstein was absolutely unique.

That's the way you can sort of look at it. To explain exactly how this works: Modern civilization, starting

from people like Nicholas of Cusa and people like that, progressing up through the ages, we have a record of progress of mankind's understanding of scientific principle. Kepler, for example, is extremely important; he's extremely important even still today. We're now in a new period where we're going into a galactic system. That is, the development of a Galactic System which man will rely on for maintaining the water supplies for mankind on Earth. These kinds of things.

So we're going through a period of revolutionary understanding of what the word "science" means. So we go through a period, up to the Twentieth Century. Now with developments in the Twentieth Century, some particularly evil people from Britain destroyed the meaning of science. And Einstein was the only man called a scientist, who had an honest understanding, of the meaning of the word "science." Other people had scientific skills, but they didn't have a comprehensive view of what the meaning of science per se means. Einstein did. And we're hoping that we can get things in that direction, for example, like the galactic question: that mankind has to, now, move out so that we depend for our water supplies, for example, in our system, on the question of the Galactic System. And that's the way it has to work.

We have not yet gotten into that; we're looking at it. And we can look into it. We're having things that are happening in China: China is moving, very advanced, relatively speaking, in terms of how the Galactic System works. It's not a fully Galactic System, but in China that work is being done as it's not being done in any other part of this planet. These are the kinds of considerations which you can explore, and pick your choice, so to speak, of what you think you would like to get at it the most.

Reverse the Degeneration of the Twentieth Century

Q5: I'm C— and I'm in San Diego. I've got two questions; you can pick and choose—one or both. What is your position on thorium reactors for nuclear power generation, or desalination? And what weak places in the imperialist structures are likely to trigger a break in confidence in their façade for this Zeus system, either domestic or international; and where is LaRouchePAC strategizing to attack?

LaRouche: Well, the first thing you've got to deal with: We've got to look at the increase of the energy-flux density represented by human capability. Like the science driver, the skills and so forth, that a human being, has the power to go to a higher level of achievement. And that means that that should be general.

The problem has been, to understand the thing relatively, that there has been, over the course of the Twentieth Century, a long road, up to the present time and so forth, of a degeneration in the intellectual capabilities of the people of the Twentieth Century.

Signs of the degeneracy of the early Twentieth Century: Banking tycoon J.P. Morgan and the pro-KKK film "The Birth of a Nation," promoted by President Woodrow Wilson in 1915.

The problem is now how are we going to face the issue of solving that problem, of getting rid of the degeneration?

For example: Look at the case of the employment of our citizens, or the *non*-employment of our citizens. What we're doing is, we are destroying the very life, and the means of life, of the citizens of the United States. You have a few diminishing numbers of privileged people—who maybe should not be privileged—who are sucking the blood out of most of our economy, of our people. That's wrong. So that our prime thing is to turn the thing around, so that the direction of mankind's advancement, in terms of the average human being, through education, through means of practice and so forth—it means now to turn around the case, so that we stop what we've been doing during the Twentieth Century, with the wars of the Twentieth Century and so forth, put in.

In other words, the Nineteenth Century was a century of progress. At the end of the Nineteenth Century, into the Twentieth Century, there became a direction of decline. And our concern must be to return to a human culture, to what it had been earlier, as in the Nineteenth Century, to turn that back, and to get mankind into a

higher level of skills, of understanding, in the scientific capabilities, for example.

Ascher: And, for our participants this evening, what Mr. LaRouche has cited is also fully documented in the new issue of *Executive Intelligence Review*, that just came out today, entitled "One Hundred Years of Stupidity: The Cesspool That Was the Twentieth Century."

Q6: My name is R— and I'm calling from upstate New York, and it's a great privilege to talk with you, Mr. LaRouche. I have a great respect for your work and the work that you've done over the many years.

We have many problems in our nation, and it seems that we've allowed our government, and our national community, to fall away from the basics, the fundamentals, that have made our country strong in the past. For example: Our advantage is, we have diversity; we have a melting pot, people from all over the world, and with different perspectives. And when we come together in a meeting of the minds, we can be stronger than the sum of our individual parts. But we ignore that. Instead of having, say, ambassadors, we now allow the military to be in the position, or the role, of the ambassador, and they don't have the same perspective, and they make serious mistakes.

There are so many problems that we could talk about, fundamental issues that are severe, and yet they're clearly evident. Your organization has talked about them and exposed many of them, and we've even come up with ideas and solutions. But what we don't have is the unifying force. The media have failed us. The media have a fundamental bias. Banking has a fundamental bias. The antitrust laws are not in effect.

So my question is, do you see any unifying event, or unifying person, in the near future, that can actually bring our country back together again, and fix all these problems?

LaRouche: Yes. I've had a very clear idea of what is actually feasible.

The problem is that the controlling forces in the United States today—including cultural forces—because our cultural forces, like the education system in science, and so forth, all kinds of things, which should be great contributions in the education of the population, and their practice—that has been largely destroyed. All you have to do is look at the deterioration of the income of the typical citizen in the United States. The conditions of life of the average citizen in the United States, have been accelerating at a downward rate, especially since, say, the beginning of the 1970s period on, or the 1980 period, more particularly.

The Bush family, for example. The Bush family's interest, and investment in our governing bodies, has been one of the chief sources of corruption of the United States up to this date. And we can only hope that we could get to see a better kind of President, which is possible. We've had good efforts, attempts, at least, to do that. That's one part.

But the other thing is that we've got to understand what mankind is. And that's what is really needed. Many people can see that this is wrong, and that's right, or may be right, but we need a better standard to measure exactly what it is we must achieve for the future of

EXECUTIVE INTELLIGENCE REVIEW

October 23-29, 1979

Volcker's Depression

U.S. ECONOMY

CLOSED

New Solidarity International Press Service $10

What happened to the American people.

mankind, in particular here in the United States—it's a good place to start, to compare it with, maybe, what's going on in Europe and so forth. But that's where we are.

We need a new definition, which means we need, actually, by our standard, a change in government. Now we have a prospect, a possible prospect, of a new Presidency coming forth in the course of the period ahead. The problem is, the danger is, that the Obama Administration will bring us into a global war, from which almost no human being will survive. If that happens—and that could happen within the next month—then you would have a situation where the question would be: Would humanity, as such, survive a general thermonuclear war—which is what we're up against? And Obama's now at the point of pushing us, on behalf of the British, of course, to get us into committing that kind of genocide against ourselves.

And so therefore, these kinds of considerations are important.

What's important, for us, above all, is to realize how we got into this mess, coming out of the Twentieth Century, and how we get out of this mess which the Twentieth Century has put us into.

Obama's Drive to Thermonuclear War

Q7: [no name given] One of the questions I want to ask you is about the crimes that Obama has committed against humanity. We already know that he did murderous crimes, treason. They've got all the evidence they need to impeach this man. I still don't understand how come everything is still being prolonged? It's like, keep him in there, and everybody's just got to wait and see what's going to happen. I feel like they've got enough evidence against him, and why don't they just get rid of him? Because you're saying that we need him out of there at least before July 4th comes—so why is he still in there? And then August comes, and he's still in there?

I just feel that they're kicking the can down the road, such as with the economy situation; as with impeaching Obama, they just keep prolonging, and kicking it down the road. When is it going to end?

LaRouche: Well, let's try to end it immediately. The possibility is there.

First of all, we're on the edge of an actual thermonuclear war throughout the planet. Right now, the United States, under the direction, or the putative direction, of Obama, is heading us for the thermonuclear war, on a global scale, within a period of probably the next month. That's the fact.

Now, that can be adjusted, that can be influenced. Actions can occur which can prevent this from occurring. But we've got to make sure that they do, that those events are straightened out as needed.

But in the longer period, [the task] is to recognize, that what happened is, in the Twentieth Century, after the Nineteenth Century, from the beginning of the Twentieth Century, there has been a long wave of ups and downs, but most of the direction is commonly *down,* in terms of the conditions of life of people. There've been formal technological capabilities introduced, but they're merely technological; they're not scientific, they're technological. And for the most part you'll find, more and more, especially since, well, shall we say 1980, there has been a more or less consistent direction of *down, worse and worse,* throughout the United States itself.

You have, however, improvements in China. China is the leading nation *in progress on the planet right now.* In other words, of all the nations of the Earth, China now has the greatest rate of progress. Now we're having in India, it's showing similar progress. Other parts of the world are showing progress of significance. In nations of South America. It's maybe not very impressive, but the very fact that it's progress is progress.

And therefore, what we have to do is focus on the *need.* We've got people who lack education, they lack skills, they lack competent employment. They lack the means of maintaining a decent life. They're no longer protected against disease, as they used to be, even before. And these things have to be done. And I think it all has to be done with one fell swoop. I think that we have to get rid of Obama. Throw him out of office, and try to get a new Presidential system.

Now, I don't think that's just *a* President. What we

Bundesregierung/Gottschalk

Barack Obama at his closing press conference at the G7 meeting in Bavaria, Germany on June 8, where he launched a new diatribe against Russia.

need is a Presidential system, in which there's a group of people, gathered around a person called the President, who's qualified to be such a President, and this team of people become the means, working together, to move the condition of life of the citizens of the United States in general—and other nations as well—in a direction which will rapidly, at an accelerating rate—bring about some kind of decent improvement in life.

And to save us from the threat that Obama now threatens. If Obama is not thrown out of office in the near future, and continues the policy he has now, we're headed for thermonuclear war. And that is probably as early as within the month. And if that is not prevented, then the problem is that most of the human species will disappear.

The Mission of the Papacy

Q8: This is B— in Wisconsin, and I have a question, actually two. What is your opinion of the Bilderberg organization? And what is your position and opinion concerning the current occupant of the papal throne, Pope Francis.

LaRouche: On the first count, I don't think much of it at all. It's a failure.

Now the case of the papacy. Discussing the papacy is a complicated matter. First of all, it reflects, on the one side, an attempt to create a Christianity which might be measured against the standard of a famous figure, Nicholas of Cusa, who was the founder of the form of Christianity which made the best contribution to mankind. And he was, of course, nominally a Catholic, but the term Catholic has come to mean a number of other things as well—in quite sharp differences.

So, the question of how mankind sees man, and sees what the meaning of human life is,—which means that, we are not animals. We human beings are not animals. Some people behave like animals, but that's not what they're supposed to do. We all live, and we all die. Now, dying is not really something we can complain about. If we think it's unjust or should not happen, or can be prevented, that's a point. But the point is, that we know in history, two things about mankind.

Korean Culture and Information Service

Pope Francis during his August 2014 pastoral visit to Korea.

First of all, no animal is capable of being a human being. No matter how sweet the animal is, how lovable the animal is, it's not human. And what we desire is to have human beings—and there are some great people. There's Vernadsky, for example, the famous Ukrainian-Russian figure, who's an example of this kind of outlook. Other people have had it—Nicholas of Cusa, of course, particularly.

So the question is, how do we solve this question? How do we say we've got the right choice?

Well, I would say that the present Pope is probably a very significant improvement over some of the things that had immediately gone on before. I don't know how good he is, but I'm sympathetic to the idea that what he will do, will be useful to mankind. And I don't limit this to the Catholic position. I look at the whole thing from the standpoint of mankind. How is the idea of religious belief, whether it's formally religious or not, what is simply the idea of what the purpose of mankind's existence is to be? And that's what the whole thing means. That's what Christianity meant. What is the meaning of human life, given the fact that every human being, sooner or later, is going to die? And most of them will die at a fairly early period.

So, what is the meaning of human life? The meaning of human life lies in the *outcome* of human lives, in the progress of mankind to accomplish good, in a very meaningful way, for the future generations of mankind. It's called progress on its own terms.

And Nicholas of Cusa is a very good example of this, and his arguments there are excellent, when it comes to the question of religious argument. This would apply, even though he's a Christian, in general to the religious conception in mankind, a proper conception, in any case. One has to think in these kinds of terms that Nicholas of Cusa exemplifies. And you will find that great scientists, and so forth, all share in that kind of intention. Because they're looking for a future of mankind, not just the future of some living person or persons.

Therefore, I think, this is the higher meaning of being human. It's that we use our lives, express our own lives, by directing our lives to the intention that we are going to do something, in the course of life, that gives mankind a step above what mankind has been able to achieve before.

The Forces of Evil and the FBI

Q9: This is B— from New York. I would like to ask, how could we go from New York to California, from Utah to Texas, Hawaii, and Alaska, to tell Americans: Truly understand the Declaration of Independence? A friend of mine and I were talking about this a few days ago, and I think that's an appropriate question to ask *true* Americans, in the situation that we [audio loss]: do you really understand the Declaration of Independence, and what it meant [to get rid of it]? And how Glass-Steagall could just throw all that in the garbage, basically? Would you elaborate on that, Mr. LaRouche?

LaRouche: Yes, quite. For me, there's a very simple standard. We have the founding of the United States under a great statesman, who actually set out the laws under which the Constitution was presented [Alexander Hamilton]. And that's still there. And the tradition is there. So, for us in the United States, that tradition is clear.

There were violations. For example, we had people who dealt in slavery in the United States. Many of the leaders of the United States in the earlier period, and later, were actually evil people. That is, they were cruel. They committed crimes against humanity of all kinds, and so forth. We finally, with some Presidents, we got free of that, and we keep struggling.

Then we fell back into it. I would say the Bush family is an example of degeneration of the United States, morally and otherwise.

It's that kind of outlook, is the one that we have to steer clear of.

Q10: This is M— from northern Nevada. My wife and I have been long-time supporters of this organization. I've attended legislative sessions in Carson City to support and encourage the passage of Glass-Steagall, the reinstituting of the national banking system of credit, the development of major infrastructure projects like NAWAPA. Over that time, I've talked with ranchers, farmers, small city and county officials, watermasters, planners, even spoken with some local journalists. I have handed out and mailed to these individuals your plan for full economic recovery, but, over the last few years, have received no response.

I believe the reason is, I don't have a sense of credibility with these people, or credentials, and therefore, they're only concerned about their own little constituency, their own small problems, or their own re-election campaign and so forth. And I'm sure there are other people, other people maybe even on this call, or who would like to ask the question: What else can an individual possibly do?

LaRouche: Well, I'm doing it, as far as I'm concerned.

EIRNS/Stuart Lewis

FBI agents at the scene of the October 6, 1986 Leesburg raid against offices associated with Lyndon LaRouche.

Look, what's happened is this. You have the FBI. It's one of the institutions that's responsible for this problem. And what they do, is they actually create a destruction of the ability of the American citizen to understand what he himself is all about. That's the problem.

Now, our organization, my organization, has been a victim of this process, and even in our own ranks, we have people who, shall we say, get stupid. And what we're doing, particularly in this discussion, which we do regularly every week at this point, is to bring into play, instead of taking a local-yokel kind of operation—which tended to be the case beforehand, to which I said, "no more, no more"—and we go to a larger constituency, meaning a broader section of the United States citizenry, in particular, and to get their voices into play here, in order to kick the butts of some of our other members who don't do the job they should do, but are still playing games with themselves.

That's what we're doing.

Now, the reason for this problem is the FBI, and the FBI's not the only institution that does it, but the FBI's notorious for this. The FBI demoralizes, in the system of demoralizing the American people in their lives. And therefore, people become confused. They become what they call "practical," rather than scientific. They say: This will be practical. And they think in small terms, and people who think in small terms, are easy victims for major institutions which manipulate the population.

Take the case of the FBI—it's typical. There are other institutions of the United States who do the same thing. And you have similar phenomena in other nations. But in the United States, the FBI has been traditionally the marker—it's not unique—but it's the marker for brainwashing citizens, by manipulating them, usually by fear, as we saw it in the post-war period.

Once Franklin Roosevelt was dead, the FBI took over, and set up a system of police-state mentality which lasted for most of that period, even under great Presidents which we had at that period. And we had Presidents who got assassinated, and these assassinations of Presidents were not coincidences. They were the elimination of Presidents like the Kennedys, the two Kennedy brothers, and other people of great talent and devotion.

Remember, for example, President Kennedy himself, faced with the threat that the Soviet Union and the United States were going to be thrust against each other, and the effect would have been—if that had happened, at that time—you would have had World War, general mass death, throughout much of the planet, including the United States! Kennedy prevented that. He induced the Soviet Union, the Soviet government, to understand what the effect of such a conflict would be. The Soviet government then said, yes, directly under Kennedy's pressure. What the Soviet government did was destroy its war machine for thermonuclear war. And that's how we survived.

Now we're at a stage, where we have Obama, who is trying to drive toward a thermonuclear war, internationally. And if Obama does that, succeeds in that, most of you will be dead on the morning following. More so than what had happened at the time when Kennedy saved the United States, and the Soviet Union, simultaneously. Under Kennedy's influence, which got Khrushchov to back off. And that's the kind of world we live in. And that's the kind of situation we have to deal with right now.

The Mission of Mankind

Q11: My name's T— and I'm from Michigan. I agree with your 24th edition's on the Darwinism versus creation ["T.H. Huxley's Hideous Revolution in Science," *EIR* #24, June 12, 2015]. I think that's been a huge problem in the United States. Very similarly, I think the degradation of the family values have been a bad thing. A lot of children growing up in broken homes, I think, has been a huge part of our crime rate in the

United States. And I was wondering what effect do you think joining the BRICS, if any, would have on those two principles?

LaRouche: Well, the problem that you're talking about, human experience, and you see it in the United States: Who are the people in the United States as citizens who are most likely to be criminals? Are they not the people who have no real vision, of creating progress for the human species? Or progress of their own community? That's the problem. Now, how does this happen?

It happens because powerful interests, in various nations, believe in suppressing their own populations by brutalizing them, making them stupid, and then letting them play their frustrations against one another.

When the proper destiny of mankind is that every human being should be steered by the aid of their society to achieve a higher standard of existence of the human species, than the generation before them. That's the intention. In other words, mankind is not an animal; mankind cannot be measured by animal standards. An animal species is a different thing than the human species, absolutely different. There is no similarity, directly, functionally, between a human being and animal, under those conditions.

And so therefore, our challenge is, *mankind must make progress.* And it's a progress of *creativity*, not opportunity, but creativity. For example, we now have, say in California, we have a governor in California, who's really a criminal, because what he's doing, is he is suppressing the clean water system of California and adjacent areas. Why should we do that?

California—you know what the history of California is. It starts out and it becomes the most powerful influence for productivity in the entire United States, in terms of foodstuffs and so forth. What happened? They're destroying it. Why? Well, because they had a couple of people like a yahoo, who came in imported from Europe and took over the governorship of California, and with that governorship of this yahoo, California began to go down. Whereas the earlier governor of California [Pat Brown] was excellent, the one whose son, his successor [Jerry Brown], is a bum, and is actually devoted to destroying and killing the members and the citizens of California!

So the issue here is not the so-called practical questions in the ordinary sense. The point is that mankind has intrinsically, a responsibility to evolve mankind's skill to achieve things that mankind has never achieved

Pacific Gas and Electric

Prosperity depends upon increasing energy-flux-density production, the basis for progress. Here, the two units of the Diablo Canyon nuclear power plant in California.

before. And that's the lesson. That's the principle of physical science: What man has never achieved before, must now be achieved. No animal can say that! No animal can do that. Only a human being. And human beings are the meaning, of the existence of the Galactic System. And once we understand that, and say, we have to develop every generation, of living human beings to be on the average, stronger, more powerful, more competent, than the generation before. Every parent, every parental family, must be enabled to achieve a higher level of achievement, than their parents had been able to do.

Bringing the BRICS to the United States

Q12: Hi, this is A— from San Diego. This is directed to Mr. LaRouche. I first found your website two years ago. My question is about the understanding among the leaders of other countries about the role of the British in international politics, in the politics of the world? How, for instance, does Putin, amongst others, view the role of Great Britain in manipulating international politics?

LaRouche: Look, Putin is Putin. He's a leader of Russia; he's a leader of Russia who has actually successfully brought Russia back up from the despairing condition it was in for a long period of time. Russia has now reached a point of progress, where it's probably

comparable, shall we say, with Germany, and Germany has a very high technology level. There are many problems in the German government's practice there, but there's a core in German culture which is a very good culture. It's probably one of the best ones in Europe in terms of performance. There are problems there, big problems, but Germany is one of the most successful of these badly mangled governments.

Now, Putin has brought Russia back up from the kind of worn-down, broken-down state it was in for a long period of time. I'm quite experienced with this Russia business. I've been involved in dealing with it one way and the other, again, so I understand it very well.

Russia is also very important, because Russia and China are actually united, in terms of collaboration. China has the largest population on the planet, of any nation, and it has the highest rate of progress, of improvement, of any nation right now. So these things are very important.

Now, what our job is, is to take examples: like Germany is a mangled, damaged, etc., thing, but it has the highest quality of performance in terms of production, in terms of economic progress of any nation in Europe. There are other, smaller nations which have good characteristics and useful, but for leading nations, Germany is now currently the most important one in Western Europe.

But you also have not only China, but India. India's one of the largest, and most powerful nations in the planet. Its population standard is not always so good, but it's going to develop very rapidly now, despite the problem of the recent heat wave they have there. But so, these are facts: Egypt has become very powerful, in its own domain.

So therefore, what we have to do is understand that, if we see these things in these terms, and say, come back to our own United States, and say: How can we make our United States, which was once a leader in the world in the achievement, how can we bring that nation, in its ruined and tattered and rotten condition it's in today, which has happened especially over the course since the beginning of the Twentieth Century—how do we save the United States? How do we save the people of the United States? How do we save the future, of the people of the United States? Hmm?

I think we can do it, but we have to have a consciousness of what that mission is. We have to have an understanding of what we're talking about. What do we have to do, to bring the United States back, out of the rubble field it has become, intellectually, and bring it again to what it was at its high point, in terms of the beginning of the Twentieth Century? And that's what we have to do.

And we have to look at nations, in terms of what's happening to nations. For a long period of time, nations have been considered as being sort of insulated, totally separate, separate from one another. Now, it's different: For example, the case of China, India, Russia and so forth, and some major nations in South America—these nations are now coming together in what's called the BRICS formation. This formation is one in which, well, the Chinese refer to it as the "win-win" concept: That every nation should have its own independent view, win; but it should also have a concern, for the influence of the other nation, win. And this thing is spreading throughout Asia—not all of Asia, but much of Asia. It's spreading in South America. It's spreading in some parts of Central America, and it should be spreading inside the United States.

If we can get Obama thrown out of office, get a competent President, or Presidency in place, instead of Obama, and we can have in the United States, its own "win-win" option, and where the United States will have the best level of achievement that it *ever* has had, so far. ...

Creating a New Presidency

Q13: F— from Louisiana. Give me a status update on Martin O'Malley, and our people working directly with O'Malley on economic policy, the Glass-Steagall, plus the physical economy? O'Malley and our staff working with him; what is the status of our staff from *EIR* working with O'Malley on the physical economy?

LaRouche: OK, OK. I understand, I know him. I

CC/Hullernuc

Under Putin, the Russian nuclear industry is expanding. Here unit one of the Novovoronezh Nuclear Plant, under construction in 2010.

don't know if that's the right term to use. What, what I see—Jeb Bush has just been sort of dumped by his own circles, because he's incompetent. Or he's admittedly incompetent, which is sort of an achievement. All the other Bushes were, except Prescott, who was a murderer—were pretty much incompetent. So, this guy has been caught with incompetence by his own circles. That's good. Get rid of this guy.

But I think that, also, there are other contenders, for the Presidency right now, who, by my understanding— my good guess, more than guess—they are not competent.

Now, what are we looking for? The O'Malley question has come up. Now, we're not talking about O'Malley as being some kind of a magic guy, who's going to solve all your problems. I think that would be a mistake, and O'Malley would understand that, as I do, more or less. The issue here is, we've got to think in terms of a Presidential System: Which means you have an actual President, with no phony stuffing; an actual President, but a President who is interacting, constantly, with a team, which is the Presidential System. Now, the Presidential System is a lot of talents, which are qualified and work together, in order to move the United States, and other things, forward.

At this point, I don't think Hillary Clinton's going to make it. She's got too many mistakes, and she has too many habits, which are mistaken. She looks like, you know, she's a big thing, right now. But, I would say, her performance is, the more people find out what she's doing, the less they're going to support her, because she's not a competent leader. She does not understand how to be a competent leader. So, I think she's sort of eliminated.

Bush is eliminated.

The retinue of the Republican Party, is a mess. There are Republicans who I would even consider—as should be considered, as part of the Presidential System. Not because they're Republicans, as such, but because they happen to be Republicans, who are worth something. Rand Paul is a tempting example of that kind of thing. Other people in that category are also tempting choices.

But, if we bring the right talents together, in the right conjunction, and we have a successful formation of O'Malley, as a Presidential candidate, I would say that is *probably*—I'm not going to give you any final answer on this thing, but I say *probably*, given the condition; knowing that Bush is in deep trouble and his own ranks are disgusted with him. And, Hillary is not going to be able to withstand reality. She may have a lot of money there, but she's not going to be able to do the job. We know that.

So, therefore, O'Malley probably is the best prospect, right now. But this does not mean O'Malley, per se. It means O'Malley, if he's chosen, will be a President who has a whole array of talents, which are working to a common purpose and a common goal, as pretty much a model, which Franklin Roosevelt had, in his term in office. A Franklin Roosevelt-like government. And that's our best option.

Now this may mean we have a foreign policy, also, which goes with the agreement with the principle which I've just referred to, the "win-win" concept. We no longer have nations which are, in themselves, dominant over large parts of the planet. We're going to have nations which work together—with their own opinions, their own experience, their own policies—but which consider other nations, with their own policies, with the idea that these different groups, which form these sets of nations, will interact to effect common ends, for mankind. Common ends for mankind. And that's what's required.

Q14: Good evening, Mr. LaRouche. This is J— from Brooklyn, New York, and my statement and my

EIRNS

Historian Robert Ingraham addresses the Schiller Institute's June 6 conference in Manhattan, on "The American Revolution and the Battle Against the Bestial Conception of Man."

question—does enter into something that you just talked about. It stems from the conference that we just had, this past weekend, and, I wasn't able to ask the question there. The conference was excellent, I thought the speakers were very good, and, of course, Helga [Zepp-LaRouche] was very inspirational. I've kind of fallen behind in my organizing, a little bit, lately, because I have some family issues—I have a new grandson, and he has medical issues, so I'm kind of dealing with that, but I was very inspired by Helga, and the other people on the panel. And I'm going to get back to it.

I am a delegate to the United Federation of Teachers, the UFT. And I, along with other people, helped get the resolution passed, through the union, for our support for Glass-Steagall, in the UFT.

Now, my concern is, that I know that we are not endorsing a candidate, a person. What we are about, is the Presidency of the United States, and what that stands for. And we have our Four Laws,[1] and our candidates, that we believe in, and we're trying to get the people of the United States on board.

The thing is—I go to delegate meetings—there are over 600 members at these delegate meetings, and they are representing over 3,000 teachers. They usually vote for things to endorse these candidates, they vote on

_____
1. Lyndon LaRouche, "The Four New Laws To Save the U.S.A.Now!, *EIR*, June 13, 2014.

whom they're going to endorse. I see that, what will probably happen, as people come out of the woodwork, and place themselves into the candidacy for President, what I see happening, is that they'll go along with Hillary; it's the "go along to get along" kind of thing. And they'll vote on endorsing Hillary, kind of like mindless foolishness.

So how will I, and others who believe as I believe, and will help bring them into reality, bring people, not just in the union, but other people in general, into reality? What types of strategies can we use, to keep people—and they know, that Hillary and others are not the people we should be endorsing, they know that, but they're delusional. And they're sheep, and they *want* to go along to get along, and we have to bring them out of that; and explain what the Presidency of the United States really is.

LaRouche: Well, now you've got the teachers union. Now the teachers union is a complex process. I think, probably, you'll find, in the Manhattan area, one of the best concentrations—from among senior teachers—I don't know about some of the younger teachers, but I do know about the senior teachers; and I know that, as a group, they have generally stood up, to try to defend what they understand as their mission, even despite a lot of pressure against them. So, I don't think there's a problem there. I think that what they are doing is right, and I think that they will automatically tend, to converge upon anything that they recognize is the proper Presidency of the United States to occur now. And, I think that's the lawful way it should occur.

But, the point is, once we understand that, and say we agree on that idea, then we have to go to work, to make sure that we are working on behalf of agreeing with that idea, not only among teachers, but among other relevant parts of society, which will come together.

The problem we've had, is we've had "wheelers and dealers." For various reasons, they get stuck into the Presidential System, because somebody's pet project, or pet candidate is involved there. We need a system, which is a pure system of the Presidency. We need a President, but the President has to conform to a certain "mission orientation," and he has to do it effectively.

But you also need a battery of people who are qualified, to do the various parts of the job, which are re-

demconvention.com

We need to create a Presidency, not submit to the "wheeler-dealers." Here, the 2012 Democratic Party convention in Charlotte, North Carolina.

quired, to make the whole thing work. And, that's exactly what we have to do. I think we can write off certainly, Bush. He's written himself off, publicly, and all of his supporters have been complaining that he's no damned good, which is probably a good term to use. I don't think the Bushes *were* any good, at any time. Prescott Bush was evil, and most of his offspring were stupid, but also evil.

But so, the point, I think we should not have really a problem, and I think that there's no resistance, *if* we can pull together the people who, of various groups, in society, who already have some idea of what this is about, get the discussion going among *those* groups: What do they want, for the people of the United States, from the standpoint of what the institutions they represent, amount to? That's the way to do it.

We need a system, a Presidency, which is a *true* Presidency. A President is there: The President's function is to lead in coordinating among a larger Presidency. The larger Presidency must work in concert with one another, in order to make this thing work.

And I think, you know, that O'Malley has shown inklings of that, or perhaps better than inklings. And I've seen nothing else, so far, on the screen, to support. So, I think, we're not going to say that O'Malley is going to be the next President. I wouldn't say that, yet. I don't have all the chips and things that I need to come to a definite conclusion. But I say, what I *do* know, is that he is the only one on the scene, who, so far, has shown the potential to become *a* President. But, that is conditional, upon having a Presiden*cy* formed. You're not trusting one man, one person; you're trusting a team of people, who are organized around a common purpose, pretty much like what a good teaching program is.

Focus on the Scientific Principles

Q15: This is J— from Middletown, New York, how are you? I first want to commend you in all your efforts, you and your whole team. I am part of this team, and proud of what we're trying to do here. And I hear a lot of different stories, or a lot of different reasoning, or resolutions, that can be potentially successful. I think ultimately, what it all boils down to, is what it's always been since the beginning of time: It's the battle between good and evil.

You can sit here, and discuss these matters for weeks, months, years even—Mr. LaRouche, you've been at it for—what? 50, 60 years? We can discuss all these different matters amongst other leaders in the world; we can go into the communities and the inner cities, and discuss these matters. And what is all boils down to, is the battle between good and evil.

What people need to realize is, what are you made of, personally? What do you have within you that's going to make a change for the better? It's unfortunate that this world is run by corrupted people. It's unfortunate that the media is controlled by these corrupted people. It's unfortunate that most people in this world live or die off of the American dollar. All that is unfortunate.

Ultimately, it means nothing. It all means nothing, because what we have inside of us, is what will ultimately lead us to our little slice of heaven, so to speak. And I get it. I get what you're saying. Yes, we do need a system. However, there's so many things that we need to take place at the same time, in order to be successful. And unfortunately, I just feel, it may be, too little too late.

I am very optimistic, and I like to think that there's always a chance. But with everything that's going on in this world, and the control that they have, literally over people's minds, with all the distractions of the social networking, and video games, and the food that we eat, that literally distorts our hormones—it's on such a massive scale, all of the evil that surrounds us.

LaRouche: That is not a problem. Not if we approach things properly. It's really not the problem. The problem is the failure to—not to deal with things that people are proposing. That's the trap. If you're trying to talk about what some people are proposing, variously, trying to pick that out, you're going to lose. Because

that kind of approach doesn't work. It's intrinsically a failure.

There are principles, however, which are knowable principles, which are little known, unfortunately, and little regarded. So, trying to come up with a *practical* solution in the usual term of practical, is wrong. You really have to deal with defining and choosing, a conception of policy which stands on its own legs.

For example, we just had this case where one of my associates originated the provision of the galactic water system. Now, what is that? That's a few people in the world who know what the galactic water system, in practical terms as well as theoretical principle terms, which I happen to be informed of—which is why I'm saying this right now. All right. So, we understand that if we have progress in civilizations—the highest level we knew about our system, was that of Kepler, Johannes Kepler. Johannes Kepler, at that time of his life, was the first man to define what the Solar System actually is. But that was only the Solar System.

What we've developed since that time, is an idea of the conception, an actual practical conception, which is called the Galactic System. That is, the water system that mankind lives on, is basically located in the Galactic System, *not* the water system as we know it, not the moisture system, as we know it. And therefore, if we want to deal with the challenges which mankind faces, as in weather conditions and so forth now, which are water conditions, then we have to approach the matter from the standpoint of galactic principles.

Now, some of my associates have been working on the question of applying the galactic principles to water throughout the planet Earth already. What they're doing so far, in practice, is modest. What they're doing in terms of principle, is serious, but requires more development. But the understanding that we are depending, *not* on the system of Earth as we see it—as we've known it before, not as known by Kepler, but as known as a Galactic System.

So, therefore, that's the kind of way you have to approach some of these problems. And that's been the case in all important scientific progress.

What we have to do is, we have to say, "What is the system, of social process, *and of* physical processes *within* social processes? What is the system that we have to use, to solve the challenges which confront mankind now?"

So, you don't come up and say, What is the pragmatic solution? The pragmatic solution went beyond

An artist's impression of Earth's home galaxy, the Milky Way.

the hope of finding success with a pragmatic solution. We have to work for an actual scientific solution, such as what is illustrated as the case, that we've now demonstrated, and a number of scientists have demonstrated this—and both in principle and in practice, we now know that the water system of Earth, of all parts of the Earth, depend on a Galactic System, not the water system of Earth itself.

And therefore, we need to approach things in that way, which is the way of *scientific principle*, actual scientific principle. And it is only an illustration I'm giving. All scientific progress depends upon the same method, as it did for Kepler in his time, as it applies now with the Galactic Principle today. And we have to look at the politics of things in terms of these kinds of considerations.

What can we do to make planet Earth, and the Galaxy, produce the effects, which mankind requires? And this means the behavior of mankind, as well as everything else. We need to have a science-driver center, which is a consulting point, like a scientific research capability, to teach us, and help us understand, what the measures are that we should be planning in our plan, for the United States, for example, today: What do we need, for the next generations? And define that thing, and say, "Okay, we're going to have a program which fits those designs." And we need that.

You can find from past history, earlier history, you can find many examples, where this thing, where the so-called practical solution, is rotten; it's a rotten failure. Where you have to have a scientific, or higher level, of understanding of mankind. And that's what we have to do. That's the only way we can guarantee that we'll produce something that will work.

Ascher: Well, Lyn, I think that your last response gives everybody on the call a clear focus of what the intervention of you and our movement has to be now, and in the upcoming period. And it brings us really to the end of our time this evening. Do you want to put any last, final touches on what you've covered tonight, because you have given everybody a tremendous amount to think about. So, did you want to add anything in conclusion here?

A Final Reflection: I'll just add one thing, a reflection: We came into the question at the close of the series of interlocutives: the education system, including in the New York City area educational system, a fairly high level of organization, is one of the best institutions for this purpose in the United States. That's a relevant example. We also need something like that, in terms of a *scientifically competent* view of what the policy of the United States would be for the benefit of the people, now, and for the future: the same thing.

We need to think in those terms, not the so-called gimmick terms. Too many Presidencies, too many politicians, come up with a gimmick, and none of these gimmicks have been successful. The territory of the United States is strewn with useless, worn-out gimmicks. We need a scientifically sound approach, for example, as the case of the water question, the relationship which first came to be understood by Kepler, and more recently, as a galactic water system. We need that kind of approach.

We are living under the Galactic System, and the Solar System as the subsidiary of the Galactic System. We therefore have to understand, how we relate to the subject of the Solar System, and Galactic System. We have to find practical problems defined, and practical solutions. That we *can do*. A competent science *can do that*. And that's what we need right now.